Turkey
West Coast

by Sean Sheehan

An experienced travel writer, Sean Sheehan has contributed to guide books to many European and Asian destinations. ... his second ... being ... ıerly an ... he now ... Cork in

Above: *Inviting beaches draw the crowds to Turkey's west coast*

AA Publishing

A fisherman on the island of Bozcaada prepares his catch

Written by Sean Sheehan
This edition updated by Melissa Shales

First published 1999
Reprinted April 1999, August 2001, August 2002
Second edition 2003. Reprinted Jan, May, Aug and Dec 2004.
This edition 2006. Information verified and updated.
Reprinted Aug 2006
Reprinted Feb and Sep 2007

Published by AA Publishing, a trading name of Automobile Association Developments Limited, whose registered office is Fanum House, Basing View, Basingstoke, Hampshire, RG21 4EA. Registered number 1878835.

A CIP catalogue record for this book is available from the British Library.

A03591

Colour separation: Keenes, Andover
Printed and bound in Italy by Printer Trento S.r.l.

Contents

About this Book

KEY TO SYMBOLS

- map reference to the maps found in the What to See section
- address or location
- telephone number
- opening times
- restaurant or café on premises or nearby
- nearest bus/tram route
- nearest train station
- ferry crossings and boat excursions
- tourist information
- facilities for visitors with disabilities
- admission charge
- other places of interest nearby
- other practical information
- ➤ indicates the page where you will find a fuller description

This book is divided into five sections to cover the most important aspects of your visit to Turkey's west coast.

An introduction to western Turkey by the author.
- Western Turkey's Features
- Essence of Western Turkey
- The Shaping of Western Turkey
- Peace and Quiet
- Western Turkey's Famous

The author's choice of the Top Ten places to see in western Turkey, each with practical information.

The two main areas of western Turkey, each with its own brief introduction and an alphabetical listing of the main attractions.
- Practical information
- Snippets of 'Did you know...?' information
- Four suggested walks
- Four suggested tours
- Two features

Detailed listings of the best places to eat, stay, shop, take the children and be entertained.

A highly visual section containing essential travel information.

Maps
All map references are to the individual maps found in the What to See section of this guide.
For example, Bodrum Kalesi has the map reference 59B1—indicating the page on which the map is located and the grid square in which the ancient castle in Bodrum is to be found.

Prices
Where appropriate, an indication of the cost of an establishment is given by **£** signs:
£££ denotes higher prices, **££** denotes average prices, while **£** denotes lower charges.

Star Ratings
Most of the places described in this book have been given a separate rating:

✪✪✪	Do not miss
✪✪	Highly recommended
✪	Worth seeing

Viewing Western Turkey

Above: *The lucky eye, protection against malign influences, is common in Turkey*
Right: *Hand-painted dolls from Alanya are a colourful example of Turkish craftwork*

Sean Sheehan's Western Turkey

The calm waters of Ölüdeniz, though banned to yachts, are ideal for cruising in smaller craft

Beaches lapped by turquoise water, rocky crags carpeted with pine trees that look down on olive groves, blue and white beehives set out on bare rocks, sunseekers relaxing on white sand beaches, antique fishing villages and ancient civilizations—the images of Turkey in the travel brochures are based on fact, and they only hint at the richness of Turkey's Aegean coast. The major resorts are Kuşadası, Bodrum and Marmaris, with Fethiye and Ölüdeniz not far behind. Here, and elsewhere, Turkey receives tens of thousands of holidaymakers each year, yet still manages to preserve its traditional, and legendary, regard for hospitality and friendliness. Turkish people are convivial and curious, homely and hospitable to a fault, and for many visitors the lasting impression they have of the country is not the food, the beaches or the ancient sites, but of the straightforward friendliness of the people they have met.

Few destinations can match western Turkey's capacity to fulfil the disparate needs of so many different kinds of visitors. If you want to dance and party till 5am and sleep in until the late afternoon, then Bodrum and other resorts are waiting to receive you. If Greek and Roman art is more to your liking, then Ephesus is just one of the many incredibly well-preserved sites waiting to be explored. Best of all, do both and find time for everything else in between.

Getting Around

Public transport in western Turkey is a dream. Coaches, buses, *dolmuşes* and minibuses go to virtually every place of interest. Very few destinations require you to use a taxi or private car. Organized tours to major sites are readily available, but you can almost always reach them easily on your own.

Western Turkey's Features

Geography

• Turkey's west coast stretches south from Çanakkale to merge with the Mediterranean off Patara some 500km (310 miles) south as the crow flies. The waters of the Çanakkale Boğazi (Dardanelles) (➤ 38) are a traditional dividing line between Europe and Asia, which makes most of western Turkey a part of Asia. The Romans regarded the region as Asia and, until quite recently, it was generally referred to as 'Asia Minor'.

People

• The population of western Turkey is remarkably homogeneous. Nearly everyone is technically ethnically Turkish, and the non-Muslim proportion of the population is just around 1 per cent.

Religion

• Virtually everyone is a Muslim, nominally at least, and mosques are commonplace, but the secular aspect of Turkish society is more obvious along the western Turkish coast than anywhere else in Turkey.

• Elsewhere in Turkey, the month-long religious festival of Ramadan (➤ 116) transforms daily life, but holidaymakers on the western Aegean coast may not even notice it is happening. Western dress and manners are commonplace.

Surprises

• Turkey is the world's only secular Muslim democracy, the second largest European force in NATO, and the only production centre outside the US for the F-16 warplane. Women received full suffrage in 1934. Turkey has more private TV stations than any other country in Europe.

East meets West

Western Turkey is a fascinating mixture, with elements of both the Middle East and Western Europe. Turkey has applied to join the European Union and after years of uncertainty amongst decision-makers in Brussels, and the Turks themselves, this now seems a more likely event than ever before.

Both Muslim minarets (below), and pagan temples, like the one at Assos (bottom), form part of Turkey's rich culture

Essence of Western Turkey

Western Turkey is steeped in 5,000 years of dramatic history, and is intoxicating for anyone with an interest in the origins of European civilization. It started here—not in Athens or Rome—when Greek colonists sailed across the Aegean to the coast of modern-day Turkey and established settlements that would nurture the first-known historians, geographers, philosophers and poets. Many inspiring ruins of this cradle of European culture still stand, alongside resort hotels, sandy beaches, watersports facilities, and discos that belt out the latest sounds as the sun rises over Homer's Troy.

A boat ride and a stroll through classical ruins are two of the popular activities when visiting western Turkey

THE 10 ESSENTIALS

If you only have a short time to visit western Turkey, or would like to get a really complete picture of the area, here are the essentials:

- **Venture into a *hamam*** (Turkish bath) and experience the bath of a lifetime, followed by an invigorating massage on the stone platform built over the oven that heats up the water (➤ 115).
- **Explore one of the ancient Greek or Roman theatres**, many of which are remarkably well preserved, built from stone into the hillside (➤ 19, 26, 52).
- **Cruise the Aegean**, if only for a day, from Bodrum, Marmaris or Fethiye, in a traditional *gület*. Bathe on an otherwise inaccessible beach and swim in the crystal-clear waters (➤ 61, 72).
- **Watch the sun set over Çannakale Boğazi (the Dardanelles)**, the narrow strait that separates Asia from Europe and has inspired lovers, poets and generals, often with tragic consequences (➤ 38).
- **Relax and talk in the street** with Turkish people, perhaps over a glass of tea or a game of backgammon, and discover their friendliness and sense of hospitality.
- **Enjoy Turkish *meze*** (appetizers, ➤ 97) with fresh bread, accompanied by a glass of *raki* (➤ 98).
- **Visit Efes (Ephesus),** Rome's renowned Asian capital, where a quarter of a million citizens once lived. Today it is one of the world's best-preserved ancient cities (➤ 19 and 41–43).
- **Go snorkelling or scuba diving**: Bodrum, Kuşadası and Marmaris are all good centres for both.
- **Go shopping in a bazaar** and be prepared to get lost: İzmir's is especially labyrinthine (➤ 104).
- **Party till dawn** at Bodrum's Disco Halikarnas (➤ 114) or one of the many other nightspots.

Above: *The carefully restored Library of Celsus at Efes (Ephesus)*

Below: *Fun on the beach at Ölüdeniz*

The Shaping of Western Turkey

2500–2000BC
Bronze Age settlement at Troy (➤ 55), reflecting the development of trade in the Aegean and the emergence of rich and powerful local rulers.

1200BC
The Greeks raze Troy, inspiring Homer's *Iliad.* In real life, the sack of Troy was probably the culmination of economic rivalry between peoples in the Aegean. Around this time, Ionians and Greek colonists begin arriving on the Aegean coast and establish settlements such as Miletos, which later become the cradle of European science and philosophy.

900–334BC
The kingdoms of Caria, Lycia, Lydia and Phrygia emerge and govern different areas of western Turkey. Lydia, ruled by King Croesus (561–46BC) at Sardis, invents coinage, but the capital is sacked by the Persians. Under Miletos, Ionian cities rise in rebellion against the Persians, but to no avail. The Persians cross the Dardanelles (➤ 38) to Greece itself but are soundly defeated. In 334BC Alexander the Great re-establishes Greek culture along the coast.

AD44–330
St. Paul preaches Christianity at Ephesus, (➤ 19). Western Asia Minor has been part of the Roman Empire since 133BC; in the second century AD Ephesus becomes the Romans' regional capital and flourishes. In AD330 Constantinople becomes the capital of the eastern Roman empire, known as the Byzantine Empire. Christianity is its official religion.

10th–12th centuries
Islam spreads across the Empire; European crusaders arrive.

1250
Commercial ambitions lead the Genoese to expand in the Black Sea and south into the Aegean. Many islands become independent Genoese principalities.

1451–1566
The Turkish Ottomans under Mehmet II capture Constantinople and rename it Istanbul. It becomes the capital of their Empire which extends to Syria, Mesopotamia, Egypt and parts of eastern Europe and North Africa. Ottoman rule reaches its height under Süleyman the Magnificent, who captures Rhodes in 1522 and Bodrum in 1523 from the Knights of St John.

Ottoman male dress from the early 19th century

1683
The limit of the Ottoman Empire is reached when the siege of Vienna fails for a second time.

1800s
Ottoman power goes into to decline as the European Great Powers are relied on to keep the Russians out.

1853–56
The Crimean War increases reliance on Western powers.

1908
The 'Young Turks' rebel against the sultanate and continuing foreign intervention.

1914–1919
Turkey allies itself with Germany in World War I, and fiercely defends the Dardanelles at Gelibolu (Gallipoli, ➤ 44) in the northern Aegean. In 1918 Turkey accepts humiliating peace terms, and the Ottoman Empire comes to an end. In 1919 the Greek army occupies İzmir and moves inland.

1919–1923
In the War of Independence (1919–1922), the Turks defeat the Greeks, who retreat to İzmir, committing atrocities along the way and abandoning the Greek inhabitants to reprisals: İzmir is partly destroyed. Greece and Turkey agree to an exchange of populations, and the Turkish Republic is declared. Mustafa Atatürk begins to westernize Turkey and make it a secular state.

Turkey's most revered leader, Atatürk, is commemorated throughout the country

1980s
The Turkish coast draws Western Europeans in search of simplicity, sun and sea.

1990s
The military repression of Kurds in the southeast of Turkey continues.

2000s
Corruption and economic mismanagement lead a disillusioned population to vote into government a pro-EU but Islamic-leaning party. 2002 sees the first-ever competitive soccer match between Turkey and Greece.

2005
Talks on settling the Cyprus question and joining the EU begin.

Peace & Quiet

In resorts such as Bodrum, where the discos and bars only *begin* to get lively around midnight, the prospects for peace and quiet may seem slim indeed. Yet even the big resort areas have secluded spots within reach. Bodrum is an ideal base from which to explore the coast and islands by boat, and the Bodrum peninsula itself is rugged in parts, and relatively unspoilt.

In the northern Aegean, the Dilek Milli Parkı (► 40) is only 30km south of Kuşadası. To make the most of this national park it helps to have your own transport. Within the park, you can climb Samsun Dağı (1,237m/4,057ft), from the village of Eskidoğanbey (preferably not in the summer months)—a wonderful way to see wildlife and the landscape. Further away from the main resorts, the Kuşcenneti National Park, just south of the Sea of Marmara, is a fantastic place for birdwatching (► 49).

Near Selçuk and accessible by public transport, the formerly Greek village of Şirince lives up to its name ('pleasantness') and makes a good base for a walk amidst peach and apple orchards in the surrounding hills. Further south, use the resort of Fethiye (► 68–9) as a base for exploring quiet villages tucked away in the countryside, but still near the coast. If you are touring outside the high season, it should not be difficult to find inexpensive accommodation in a *pansiyon* (such as Anita & Ned's ► 102), with home-cooked food and family hospitality.

In the northern Aegean, the islands of Gökçeada (► 45) and Bozcaada (► 37) are quiet and feel very remote from the more developed parts of the Turkish Aegean. Bozcaada is smaller, but is best for solitary country walks and near-deserted beaches.

Bird Life

Reserves such as the Dilek Milli Parkı have the most species, but you will see birds almost everywhere. Storks build their immense nests on tall buildings; eagles, buzzards and vultures soar overhead. On walks through agricultural land anywhere along the coast look for the crested lark on the soil and, overhead on telephone lines, colourful bee-eaters and blue rollers. The wild flowers are fantastic too.

Bafa Gölü (Lake Bafa)

This bird and wildlife area became a Nature Park and National Park in 1994. A good accommodation base is the village of Kapıkırı, near ancient Herakleia (► 45). Some of the *pansiyons* here can arrange guides for trekking expeditions into the hills (► 100). For general information, write to PO Box 18, Bebek, 80810 Istanbul or check out www.milliparklar.gov.tr.

Above: *A short-toed eagle*
Right: *you can get away from the crowds*
Inset right: *Sunset over Bafa Gölü (Lake Bafa)*

Western Turkey's Famous

Reading Homer
Both the *Iliad* and the *Odyssey* would be appropriate reading on a visit to western Turkey, and there are numerous translations to choose from. In the 1960s Richard Lattimore translated both books in verse form and in 1990 another American, Robert Fagles, brought out an acclaimed new translation of both works. Both these translations are available in paperback.

Homer (*c*8th century BC)

Homer's epic poems, the *Iliad* and the *Odyssey*, are the foundation stones of European literature. Homer's birthplace is most likely to have been Smyrna, now the modern city of İzmir. Strabo, who hailed from Tralles (Aydın, ➤ 35), writing his *Geography* in the 2nd century AD describes a shrine and statue of the poet erected in the city. Virtually nothing is known about Homer, and even his existence has been disputed, but it is now generally agreed that the *Iliad* and *Odyssey* were compiled from older compositions in the second half of the eighth century BC. The *Iliad* tells the story of the seige of Troy (➤ 55), which lasted for ten years, until the Greeks entered the city with the help of guile and a wooden horse. The *Odyssey* recounts the adventures of Odysseus as he struggles to make his way home after the war.

The great historian Herodotus grew up in one of the many colonies established on the Aegean coast of modern-day Turkey

Herodotus (*c*490–*c*425BC)

The 'father of history' was born at the start of the 5th century BC in Halicarnassos (Bodrum, ➤ 58). He travelled extensively, not only along the Aegean coast, but also in Greece, Egypt, Persia (Iran) and parts of Italy. The subjects of his *Histories* are the wars between Greece and Persia, and along the way he provides fascinating information about the kingdoms that ruled Asia Minor before the Persians arrived on the scene. He was particularly fascinated by the Lydians and their fabulously rich king, Croesus, whose capital was at Sardis. In one of his anecdotes Croesus has been captured by the Persian king Cyrus, and asks what the Persian soldiers are doing to Sardis. 'Plundering it', smirks Cyrus, 'and confiscating all your wealth.' Croesus replies, 'Not mine, my friend, it is your wealth now that they are stealing,' whereupon Cyrus brings the plundering to a quick finish.

Top Ten

Above: *The theatre at Hierapolis can be explored in detail*
Right: *The famous statue of Artemis from Ephesus*

1
Afrodisias Stadium

30C2

40km (12 miles) southeast of Nazilli, off the main Aydın–Denizli road

Daily 8–7, summer; daily 8–5.30, winter

Anatolia Restaurant, Geyre Kasabası (££) on the road to Karacasu, 13km (8 miles) to the west

Dolmuş/minibus from Karacasu or Nazilli

None

Inexpensive

Afrodisias (➤ 34)

Tours from Kuşadası and other resorts

The stadium at Afrodisias was hidden for centuries until archaeologists unearthed the entire site

Stadia adorn many of Turkey's ancient sites, but none can compare with the one at Afrodisias, which is the best-preserved example of its kind.

The word 'stadium' comes from a measurement of about 200m (656ft), the distance of the shortest foot race in ancient Greece and which over time came to be used for the public arena where races and other games took place. The stadium of Afrodisias stretches for just over 263m (863ft) and its 25 rows of seats could accommodate 30,000 spectators. Its excellent state of preservation owes a great deal to the Turkish professor Kenan Erim and his team at New York University, who effectively resurrected Afrodisias between 1961 and his death in 1990. The stadium had been buried as a result of earthquakes in the Middle Ages and from the 13th century onwards the whole of Afrodisias had been abandoned and more or less forgotten about by the world.

It is best to follow the path that leads round the site, going first to the theatre and then to the Odeon and Temple of Aphrodite on the right. A little way past this the path heads north for 200m (656ft) to reach the spectacular stadium. The Romans were keen to emulate the Greek tradition of holding sporting and artistic competitions to mark religious festivals and the impressive scale of this stadium shows how much importance was attached to public entertainment.

The stadium was the scene of a major festival and sporting competitions, and as well as the traditional Greek events—foot races, wrestling, boxing and pentathlon—the Romans also staged chariot races and gladiatorial combats.

2
Bodrum Kalesi (Castle of St. Peter, Bodrum)

This grand example of 15th-century crusader architecture dominates Bodrum harbour and houses the Museum of Underwater Archaeology.

Bodrum's harbour is dominated by the castle on its rocky promontory

The Knights Hospitallers of St. John, militant anti-Muslim Christians, arrived in Bodrum in 1402 and set about choosing a site for a mighty fortress. The first of its double curtain walls was completed in 1437, but building work continued until 1522; shortly thereafter the Knights were forced to evacuate because Süleyman the Magnificent captured their headquarters in Rhodes. Inside the main castle there were separate towers for the English, French, Italian and German contingents, each proudly displaying its own coat of arms.

The Underwater Archaeology Museum contains an invaluable collection of some of the world's oldest ships, such as the 14th-century BC Uluburun Wreck. The Glass Wreck Hall (separate admission charge) contains a carefully preserved seventh-century Byzantine trading ship alongside its cargo of glass. The *Carian Princess* (separate admission charge) is named after the royal resident of a sarcophagus that was discovered in 1989. Dating back to *c*360BC it is suggested she was the wife or sister of Mausolus. The English Tower has been restored in a mock-medieval style. Armour and trophies decorate the walls, and staff in medieval costumes sell glasses of wine.

Climb to the top of the castle, above the *Carian Princess* room, for wide views of Bodrum and the harbour. A morbid area includes the dungeons, restored and embellished with ghoulish scenes and sound effects.

- 58B1
- Bodrum, behind the tourist information office
- 0252 316 2516; www.bodrum-museum.com
- Tue–Sun 8.30–12, 1–5 (longer hours in Jul and Aug). Shorter hours for some exhibits
- Café (£) inside the castle; many on quay outside
- Limited access. Video-show room for visitors with disabilities
- Moderate to expensive, depending how many sections are visited
- Bodrum (► 58–62)

3
Çeşme

The resort town of Çeşme has preserved its Turkish heritage

A low-key, relaxing resort on the coast, with Ottoman architecture and thermal springs, Çeşme has managed to avoid the worst excesses of tourism.

- 30A3
- 80km (50 miles) west of İzmir
- Castle and museum Daily 8.30–7.30
- Restaurants (£–££) along the seafront
- *Dolmuş*/minibus from İzmir
- Greek island of Chios, 9km offshore
- Near the pier
  0232 712 6653
  Jul–end Sep Mon–Fri 8.30–7; Oct–end Apr daily 8.30–12, 1–5
- Castle and museum inexpensive
- İzmir (➤ 31–33), Siğacik (➤ 54)

Many of the houses close to Çeşme's seafront are well-preserved 19th-century homes, and an evening wander through the streets is very rewarding. The word *çeşme* (pronounced *chesh-ma*) means 'fountain', and a number of old Ottoman fountains still exist in the town. People come to Çeşme for its water: there are therapeutic thermal springs in the area and you can benefit from these at some of the local hotels. Delightful decorated balconies adorn many of the Ottoman buildings, and there are two 18th-century mosques. A 16th-century Ottoman fortress dominates the town and is now home to a small, rather uninspiring museum.

Çeşme is not as blatantly touristy as resorts like Bodrum and Kuşadası, but the town has still developed a modest entertainment infrastructure for visitors. Any of the agencies dotted around town can arrange a day trip to Hĝos (Chios), and a longer trip to Italy via Brindisi is also possible. There is a Turkish bath in the centre of town, and although Çeşme itself is quiet at night, the surrounding area has a number of lively discos (➤ 113) and pubs.

Ilica, just 4km (2.5 miles) to the east, is the liveliest place for evening entertainment, has several excellent spas and also has the best beach in the vicinity. The beach at Boyalık is more exposed, but hot springs in the seabed help compensate for any chill in the air.

4
Efes (Ephesus) Theatre

This great Roman theatre had seating for 24,000. From the top row there is an unsurpassed view of ancient Ephesus.

A detail from the decoration behind the stage at Ephesus

In the AD60s a real life drama was played out here when St. Paul's preaching sparked off an anti-Christian demonstration (Acts 19:24–41). A pagan silversmith named Demetrius accused the Christians of disrespect for the goddess Artemis and a riot broke out. Paul left shortly afterwards, leaving Demetrius and others to recover their trade in Artemis merchandise. Their successors may be seen peddling Artemis schlock in the many stalls that line the entrance to Ephesus.

In classical Greece, theatres had no stage: all the action took place in the orchestra. In Hellenistic times a small stage was introduced, and the Romans doubled this in size to some 6m (20ft) in depth. Hence the decorated double row of columns and single row of pilasters, which are still standing—they once supported the stage.

From the stage area, with its various entrances, it is clear how the auditorium gradually gets steeper, designed as it was to provide good views for those in the inexpensiveer seats at the back. In the auditorium itself, listen to people talking in the stage area: the acoustics are still excellent, though the Greeks and Romans also placed bronze and clay sounding boards at strategic spots. From the higher rows there is a superb view of the road now known as the Arcadian Way. The reedy grass at its far end indicates what was once the line of the harbour.

- 30B3
- 3km (2 miles) from Selçuk
- 0232 892 6402/6940
- Daily 8–6.30 (5.30 in winter)
- Restaurants (not recommended) at the Lower Entrance. Bring a picnic or eat in Selçuk (► 53)
- Buses to Selçuk from Kuşadası and İzmir. Taxis and free shuttles drive up to the top for an easier walk down through the site
- (► 53) None
- Expensive
- Selçuk (► 53), Meryemana (► 50), Kuşadası (► 46–47)
- Tours from most resorts

5
Hierapolis

30C3

Pamukkale, 19km (12miles) north of Denizli

Museum Tue–Sun 9–12, 1.30–5. Rest of site open 24 hours, but no light at night

Café by Antique Pool for drinks and snacks (£)

Dolmuş/minibus from Denizli every 20 mins, long-distance bus from Marmaris, Kuşadası, Fethiye and other towns

Opposite the museum
0258 272 2077
8–12,1.30–5.30 (1.30–5 in winter)

None

Moderate

Pamukkale (► 22–23), Laodikeiá (► 49)

The huge theatre at Hierapolis is a dramatic statement in its own right

Roman architecture on a grand scale dominates Hierapolis. The theatre is vast, and the necropolis was one of the biggest in Asia Minor.

The King of Pergamum (► 24), Eumenes II, developed Hierapolis in the second century BC, but the monuments that attract visitors today were constructed by the Romans after they inherited the town. The name means Holy City, and the town was associated from the start with the mysterious Springs of Pamukkale (► 22–3), part of the same site. To appreciate the scale of the Roman theatre, take a seat in the very top row. Go down into the theatre orchestra, which gives access to the fine reliefs behind the stage. The lower ones can be admired at close quarters.

After leaving the theatre, if time permits, turn to the right and continue up the unpaved track to pass remains of the city walls, before turning left for the ruins of the Martyrion of St. Philip. If time is limited, head back to the car park from the theatre and turn right to reach the colonnaded Frontinus Street. This splendidly preserved Roman street begins just after the Motel Koru on the other side of the road. Frontinus Street is 4m (13ft) wide and at the north end has a monumental gate, dedicated to the emperor Domitian in AD84. As you walk towards the Domitian Arch look for the well-preserved Roman public toilets on the right. Continue through the Domitian Arch to the large necropolis, dotted with lavish tombs. The Roman baths contain a museum.

6
Ölüdeniz

The soft, sandy beach, with a backdrop of pine-forests, is over 3km (2 miles) long, and the water in the lagoon is transparent—avoid high season.

30C1

15km (9 miles) south of Fethiye

Restaurants (£–££) fronting the beach

Dolmuş/minibus from Fethiye

None Paying beach (inexpensive)

Fethiye (➤ 68–69)

The name of Turkey's most beautiful beach setting means 'dead sea', referring to the calmness of the water, which is almost completely cut off. Ölüdeniz is a warm, sheltered lagoon that manages to be magnificent, despite the lack of a view of the open sea and overdevelopment of the surrounding hills. At the height of summer it is packed with people; out of season, there is little that can compare. The setting is superb: the beaches stretch for such a distance that it is usually possible to find some space. The prettiest stretch of beach winds around the lagoon, but it is closed off and requires a separate entrance fee. This beach proves popular with Turkish families, while other holidaymakers seem to prefer the long stretch of Belceğiz.

Despite the popularity of Ölüdeniz, some efforts have been made to preserve the pristine beauty of its waters. Yachts are forbidden to use its sheltered location, and an attempt has been made to contain the most rampant development of giant resorts; most local hotels are relatively low key. Nevertheless, hotel advertising boards spoil the approach to Ölüdeniz from Fethiye.

The protected water of the lagoon is ideal for safe canoeing and kayaks are readily available for hire. At night, there is plenty of opportunity for partying at nightspots in nearby Ovacik and Hisarönü, but the food scene is dismal, despite the proliferation of restaurants. Take a picnic lunch if going for the day.

The beauty of Ölüdeniz is no longer a secret

7
Pamukkale

30C3

19km (12 miles) north of Denizli

0258 261 3393

Café serving drinks and snacks by the Antique Pool; otherwise picnic or eat in Karahayit village

Dolmuş/minibus from Denizli every 20 mins, long-distance bus from Marmaris, Kuşadası, Fethiye and other towns

The spring pool that attracted the Romans is now part of a motel. Swim here amongst the submerged columns of an ancient portico.

Hot spring water cools as it comes to the surface on the edge of a plateau, some 100m above the Lycos Valley, and as the dissolved calcium bicarbonate gives off carbon dioxide, the remaining calcium carbonate solidifies. The prosaic chemistry does scant justice to the place: what it means is that the water runs down a series of bright white terraces of precipitated chalk formed into irregular pools, odd shapes and stalactites.

From the valley below, you see the high plateau swathed on one side with white cliffs. Hence the name Pamukkale, or 'cotton castle'. On the plateau above the ancient town of Hierapolis developed because of the springs, which were considered holy, and the Romans established a health spa. So many visitors have followed in their footsteps that measures have belatedly been taken to protect the natural formation. Tourists are only permitted to paddle in one small area, without shoes, but there are still obvious signs of deterioration in the pools.

The calcified waterfalls of Pammukale form a remarkable natural phenomenon

Stay a night to take in the strange beauty of the place as evening falls. The Antique Pool is truly remarkable, containing a collection of fallen masonry from ancient Hierapolis (➤ 20). Get here early to enjoy a swim before the afternoon tour buses arrive and disgorge a flood of visitors.

Opposite the museum ☎ 0258 268 6539/ 272 2077 Daily 8–12, 1.30–7.30 (1.30–5.30 in winter)

None

Moderate

Hierapolis (➤ 20), Laodikeiá (➤ 49)

Tours combining Pamukkale and Hierapolis from most major resorts

Left: *It's difficult to resist taking a dip in the historic and therapeutic waters*

8
Pergamum

The dramatically steep acropolis at Pergamum has 80 rows of seats

The two great attractions here are the acropolis, a majestic statement of political might, and the Asklepeion, devoted to the art of healing.

30B4

Acropolis: 6km (4 miles) north of Bergama. Asklepeion: 2km (1 mile) south of Bergama

Acropolis and Asklepeion; daily 8.30–7 (closes 5.30 in winter)

Restaurants (£) in Bergama

Buses to Bergama from Ayvalık and İzmir

0232 631 2851 (Bergama Tourist Office) Daily 8.30–7, summer; Mon–Fri 8.30–12, 12.30–5.30, winter

None

Inexpensive

Bergama (➤ 37)

Pergamum emerged as a powerful force in Hellenistic times but the last king, Attalus III, was so keen to placate the Romans that he bequeathed the kingdom to Rome in 133BC. It remained an important city and today there is plenty to see. An organized tour that includes transport and a guide is a good bet because the acropolis is 8km (5 miles) from the Asklepeion, and both sites contain several points of interest. Otherwise, take a taxi from one site to the other and invest in a specialist guidebook (➤ 89).

On the acropolis, the Greek theatre is unusually steep, with 80 rows of seats carved into the hillside. Post holes to the rear of the orchestra still show where temporary scenery was erected as a backdrop to the drama. The partly restored Temple of Trajan evokes the grandeur of the site under the Romans but its art treasures, the relief carvings on the Temple of Zeus, were moved to the Pergamon Museum in Berlin in the 19th century.

At the far end of the modern town of Bergama, the Asklepeion was the leading medical centre of the ancient world. Patients slept in the sanctuary, hoping to be cured by divine influence, and had their dreams interpreted by priestly physicians who prescribed baths in the sacred water that still flows here. The remains of a circular temple to Zeus are worth seeing, and there is a small, well-preserved theatre in the northwest corner. In the southwest corner are remains of the public latrines.

9
Rock Tombs, Fethiye

The ancient Lycian people left tantalising traces. When an earthquake flattened Fethiye in 1957, the Lycian rock tombs remained intact.

Fethiye stands on the site of the Lycian port of Telmessos. All that remains of the ancient town is its tombs, cut into the rock overlooking Fethiye. Try to visit near sunset when the climb up is less exhausting and when there is the bonus of panoramic views. Steep steps lead up to the most impressive site, the Tomb of Amyntas, a temple-like structure with twin Ionic columns between two pilasters adorned with rosettes at the top. A fading inscription on the left pilaster records that the tomb belonged to Amyntas, and gives the name of his father. Nothing else is known about the family or the fourth century BC building. The main chamber has a door with four panels, which still have their original iron studs, although tomb robbers have broken in at some time in the past. The iron studs are imitations of the bronze nails which adorned the wooden porches of Greek temples.

30C1

Fethiye

Daily 8.30–sunset

Restaurants in town (£–££) and a café (£) opposite the entrance

Buses to Fethiye from Bodrum, Denizli, İzmir, Marmaris, Ölüdeniz, Pamukkale, Patara

(➤ 69)

Inexpensive

Fethiye (➤ 68–69)

The Tomb of Amyntas has a pillar close to collapse

10
Xanthos, Harpy Tomb

30C1

Just north of Kınık, 63km (40 miles) from Fethiye

May–end Oct daily 8–7; Nov–end Apr daily 8–5.30

Café (£) across the road but best to bring a picnic

Dolmuş/minibus from Fethiye or Kalkan

None

Inexpensive

Xanthos (➤ 90), Letoön (➤ 77), Kalkan (➤ 75), Pınara (➤ 85), Tlos (➤ 88), Sidyma (➤ 88)

The ruins of the Roman theatre and the Harpy Tomb in the background (right) alongside a twin sarcophagus

British 'archaeologists' took two months in 1842 to pillage Xanthos of its art treasures, but the site is still capable of stirring the imagination.

Start your visit to this ancient city by taking a seat in the Roman theatre, and gazing down on the orchestra, which is still full of fallen masonry from the stage and its columned façade. The experience evokes an impressive feeling for the history of the site.

To the west of the theatre stand two Lycian pillar tombs, the Harpy Tomb (545BC) and, alongside it, a twin sarcophagus. The bas-relief at the top of the 5m- (16-ft) high pillared Harpy Tomb carries plaster copies of the marble originals, now in the British Museum in London. They show seated figures receiving gifts, with bird-like, winged women carrying children in their arms on the north and south sides. These images were once thought to represent the mythical creatures known as Harpies, hideous winged monsters, personifying hurricanes and tornadoes (in Greek the word means 'snatcher'). Modern theories tend to suggest, however, that they are actually carvings of the Sirens, part women, part birds, who lured seafarers to their deaths with their enchanted singing. Here they are carrying away dead souls in the form of children. The, adjacent, twin sarcophagus dates from the third century BC. It is not known why the tombs were put on top of each other in this unusual manner.

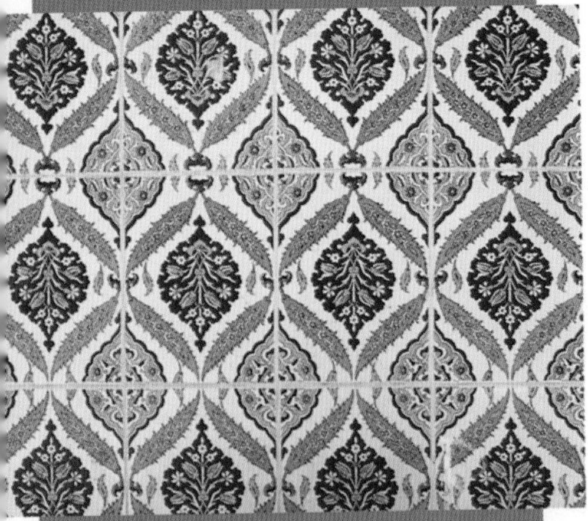

What to See

Visitors to the west coast are welcomed by Turkish people

Northern Aegean

There is so much to see. The chief resort is Kuşadası, one of the liveliest anywhere along the Turkish coast and well placed for day trips to major sites such as Ephesus, Pamukkale and Hierapolis. The city of İzmir (ancient Smyrna) is attractive, though somewhat hectic. It is a good place in which to experience the urban Turkish culture that resort towns lack. İzmir is also a convenient base for a visit to the idyllic Temple of Artemis, near the site of ancient Sardis, home to the fabulously rich Croesus in the sixth century BC. To the north of İzmir is ancient Pergamum, easiest to visit on an organized tour. Further north again lies the town of Çanakkale, which overlooks the Dardanelles, prominent in history and mythology. The World War I battlefields of Gallipoli are just across the water, and Homer's Troy is just a short day trip away inland.

'Three and four times happy
shall those men be hereafter
Who shall dwell on Pagus
beyond the sacred River'

Advice from the oracle of Apollo after
Alexander the Great suggested
founding the new city of Smyrna

Village life retains a healthy indifference to tourism

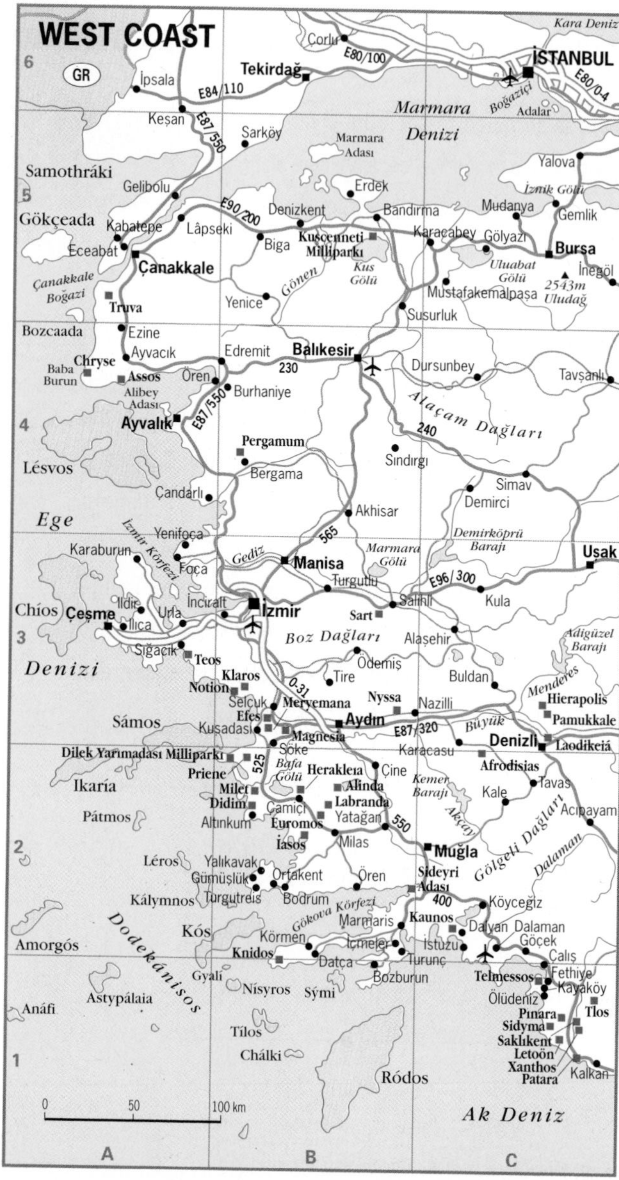
WEST COAST
Kara Deniz
Çorlu
E80/100
İSTANBUL
GR
Tekirdağ
İpsala
E84/110
E80/0-4
Boğaziçi
Marmara
Adalar
Keşan
E87/550
Şarköy
Marmara Adası
Denizi
Samothráki
Yalova
Gelibolu
Erdek
İznik Gölü
E90/200
Denizkent
Bandırma
Mudanya
Gökçeada
Kabatepe
Lâpseki
Kuşcenneti Milliparkı
Karacabey
Gölyazı
Gemlik
Eceabat
Biga
Bursa
Çanakkale
Kuş Gölü
Uluabat Gölü
İnegöl
Çanakkale Boğazi
Gönen
2543m Uludağ
Truva
Yenice
Mustafakemalpaşa
Susurluk
Bozcaada
Ezine
Ayvacık
Edremit
Balıkesir
Chryse
Baba Burun
Assos
Ören
230
Dursunbey
Tavşanlı
Alibey Adası
Burhaniye
E87/550
Alaçam Dağları
4
Ayvalık
240
Pergamum
Sındırgı
Lésvos
Bergama
Simav
Çandarlı
Demirci
Akhisar
Ege
Yenifoça
İzmir Körfezi
565
Demirköprü Barajı
Karaburun
Gediz
Manisa
Marmara Gölü
Uşak
Foça
Turgutlu
E96/300
Chíos
Ildir
İnciraltı
İzmir
Salihli
Kula
Çeşme
Urla
Sart
Ilıca
3
Boz Dağları
Alaşehir
Adigüzel Barajı
Sığacık
Teos
Ödemiş
Denizi
Klaros
Tire
Buldan
Menderes
Notion
0-31
Selçuk
Meryemana
Nyssa
Nazilli
Hierapolis
Efes
Aydın
Pamukkale
Sámos
Kuşadası
Magnesia
E87/320
Büyük
Denizli
Laodikeia
Dilek Yarımadası Milliparkı
Söke
Karacasu
525
Priene
Bafa Gölü
Herakleıa
Çine
Afrodisias
Ikaría
Milet
Alinda
Kemer Barajı
Tavas
Didim
Labranda
Kale
Pátmos
Çamiçi
Yatağan
Akçay
Acıpayam
Altınkum
Euromos
550
Gölgeli Dağları
İasos
Milas
2
Muğla
Léros
Yalıkavak
Dalaman
Gümüşlük
Ortakent
Ören
Sideyri Adası
Kálymnos
Turgutreis
Bodrum
400
Köyceğiz
Gökova Körfezi
Marmaris
Kaunos
Dalyan
Dalaman
Kós
Körmen
Göçek
Amorgós
Dodekánisos
Knidos
İçmeler
İstuzu
Çalış
Datça
Turunç
Fethiye
Gyalí
Bozburun
Telmessos
Kayaköy
Nísyros
Sými
Ölüdeniz
Anáfi
Astypálaia
Pınara
Tlos
Sidyma
Tílos
Saklıkent
Letoön
1
Chálki
Xanthos
Ródos
Patara
Kalkan
0
50
100 km
Ak Deniz
A
B
C
6
5

İzmir (Smyrna)

The third largest city in Turkey, home to nearly three million people and twinned with Cuba's Havana, İzmir has a long and illustrious past. Homer (► 14) is said to have lived here in the ninth century BC. The town was destroyed by the Lydians and lay in ruins for over 300 years, but it came back to life when Alexander the Great founded a new city on the summit of Mount Pagus.

Modern İzmir's heyday was in the 19th century when the city was both a major trading port and a cosmopolitan meeting place for merchants from the East and West. It became the focal point of the Greek–Turkish struggle in the War of Independence that followed World War I. When the Turkish army took the city in 1922 the Greek area was set on fire and three-quarters of İzmir burned to the ground. What the visitor sees today is a very modern metropolis, with a very Turkish bazaar that should not be missed (► 33). Two museums give a good introduction to the city's ancient and more recent past (► 32 and 33). Another tangible reminder of the past is Mount Pagus, where Alexander the Great was resting after a hunt when a goddess descended and urged him to found a new city. From the top of the hill there is a dramatic view of the city and the great sweep of a bay that continues to make İzmir the major port on the Aegean.

30B3
Kultur ve Turizm İl Müdürlügü, Akdeniz Mah 1344 Sik No. 2, Pasaport, İzmir 0232 483 6216/5117; www.izmirturizm.gov tr

Bottom: *İzmir is a large, modern city, but its old quarter* (below) *is worth exploring*

What to See in İzmir

AGORA

30B3
816 Sokak
0232 425 5354
Daily 8.30–5.30, summer; daily 9–12, 1–5, winter
None
Inexpensive

The Roman *agora* (marketplace) was built by Emperor Marcus Aurelius, after an earthquake in AD178 had destroyed the original one founded by Alexander the Great. A Corinthian colonnade is the main focus of interest, and items discovered here are on display in the Archaeological Museum.

ARCHAEOLOGICAL MUSEUM

30B3
Bahri Baba Park
0232 489 0796
Tue–Sat 8.30–5.30, summer; (closes as 4.30 in winter)
Café (£) in the museum
None
Inexpensive

Greek and Roman statues, monuments and parts of friezes found in and around İzmir fill this excellent purpose-built museum. There are large examples of Roman funerary monuments downstairs, but the more interesting pieces of art are on the ground and upper levels. The examples of Greek archaic art include a fine *kore* (a maiden), while Hellenistic art is represented by a statue of Eros.

ETHNOGRAPHIC MUSEUM

30B3
Bahri Baba Park
0232 484 2592
Tue–Sat 8.30–4.30, closes for lunch in winter
None
Inexpensive

The first floor includes examples of domestic Ottoman architecture, a reconstructed old pharmacy, a display on the making of blue beads for warding off the evil eye, and exhibits on the art of camel-wrestling and rope-making. The second floor has a reconstructed Ottoman bridal chamber, a 19th-century living room, a circumcision room, and displays of carpets and weapons.

KONAK

30B3
Pedestrianized
Free
Bazaar closed Sun

This central square near the seafront is the most attractive corner of the city. It has an ornate clock tower, presented to the city in 1901 by the Sultan, and opposite stands a delightful little mosque, enlivened by ornate enamelled tiles. İzmir's two main museums are just a short distance up the hill and the bazaar is also close by.

An ancient mosque in the heart of İzmir

Old İzmir

Start in Cumhuriyet Meyanı, on the waterfront near the statue of Atatürk.

Walk along the seafront to the tourist office for a town map. Continue along to the Pier. Turn left onto Fevzi Paşa Bulvari and walk up to the next main junction with Gaziosmanpaşa where there is a white-on-brown sign for the agora (➤ 32). There is a small police station on the corner. From the agora, return to the main road and cross at the traffic lights, walking straight on into Anafartalar Caddesi.

This is the main artery running through İzmir's bazaar (➤ 104). There are side-streets to explore, and it is easy to lose your sense of direction among the crowds.

Stay on Anafartalar Caddesi, which bears left after 200m (220yds), and walk down it for about five minutes. Pass by a new mosque on the right, then a dilapidated-looking one on the same side. The road bears left here again and leads into the plaza-like square of Konak (➤ 32). Turn left into the square and walk to the end, past the AKM department store.

At the end of this square is the Efes pub, on the right, and, opposite, İzmir's two best museums (➤ 32).

You can reach the top of Mount Pagus from here by taking the No.33 bus to Kadifekale.

Distance
5km (3 miles)

Time
3–4 hours, depending on museum visits and shopping

Start point
Cumhuriyet Meydanı
30B3
63, 114, 118 (from train station), 53, 61, 257 (from bus station)

End point
Konak bus station
30B3

Lunch
Efes pub (£)
7 SSK Işanı, Konak
0232 484 7036

People live traditional lives and work at Kadifekale on top of Mount Pagus

What to See in the Northern Aegean

AFRODISIAS ✪✪✪

30C2
40km (25 miles) southeast of Nazilli, off the main Aydın–Denizli road
Daily 8–7, summer; daily 8–12, 1–5, winter
Restaurants (£–££) in Karacasu, 13km (8 miles) to the west (➤ 16)
Dolmuş/minibus from Karacasu or Nazilli
None
Stadium of Aphrodisias (➤ 16)
Inexpensive
Tours from Kuşadası and other resorts

This ancient site was associated with fertility cults from as early as the Bronze Age, and the Greeks named it Aphrodisias after their goddess of love, Aphrodite. A temple dedicated to her stood here in the eighth century BC. The Romans transformed Aphrodisias into a major cultural centre, and held sculpture competitions: sculptors were especially attracted to the place because of the quality of local marble.

Parts of the site are periodically closed off for restoration work, but enough is always left open to make a visit rewarding. There is a stadium (➤ 16), a well-preserved Roman theatre, the Baths of Hadrian complete with floor tiles, and the Temple of Aphrodite, which survived its conversion into a basilica during the Byzantine era. Leave time to visit the museum with its extensive collection of sculptures.

ALİNDA ✪

30B2
25km (15.5 miles) to the west of the Aydın–Muğla main road
Restaurants (£) in Karpuzlu
Dolmuş/minibus from Aydın
None
Inexpensive
Aydın (➤ 35)

This little-visited ancient site has impressive ruins, and the setting, on the steep eastern slopes of Mount Latmus, is delightful. Alexander the Great came here and helped the Queen of Halicarnassus (Bodrum, ➤ 58–62), then in exile, regain her throne in 334BC. The chief ruin is a huge and remarkably well-preserved market building. Higher up, the small theatre is overgrown but has also survived well. It is worth seeking out for an unrivalled view over the village of Karpuzlu and the pretty valley formed by the River Çine Çayı. Higher still is a watch-tower, surrounded by tunnels, partly open, that lead down the hillside.

ASSOS ✪✪

30A4
75km (46.5 miles) south of Çanakkale, off the main Çanakkale–Edremit road, next to village of Behramkale
Daily 8–7, summer; daily 8–5, winter

The ruins of the city of Assos stand on a cliff above the pretty fishing port of Behramkale. Founded by Greek colonists in the eighth century BC, Assos was so renowned as an intellectual centre that the philosopher Aristotle lived here for three years. The town was later captured by his pupil, Alexander the Great. The highlight is the partly reconstructed Temple of Athena (530BC) with its spectacular view of Lesbos, the starting point of the original Greek colonists. There are also well-preserved sections of the fourth century BC city walls, over 12m (39ft) high in places, and a necropolis with an assortment of sarcophagi. The severe looking mosque by the side of the site dates back to the 14th century. It is well worth wandering through Behramkale to admire the fine old Ottoman bridge, built with stone from the ancient site, and the pretty harbour. There are hotels to suit most budgets, and an overnight stay is worth considering. The beach is pebbly but clean.

Hotel restaurants (£–££) in Behramkale
Dolmuş/minibus from Ayvacik (not to be confused with Ayvalık)
None
Inexpensive
Chryse (► 38)

AYDIN

Known in ancient times as Tralles, Aydın today is a busy provincial town with little of intrinsic interest. It is a useful transport point, however, if you want to catch a *dolmuş* east to Nyssa or south to Alinda. If you have time to spare it is worth taking a look in the small archaeology and ethnology museum, west of the park and square that forms the centre of town. Also near the park is an interesting 17th-century mosque. The bus station is over half a kilometre south of the town centre, just off the main road.

30B3
50km (31 miles) east of Kuşadası
Restaurants (£)
Dolmuş/minibus from Kuşadası, Pamukkale, Selçuk and İzmir
Just east of the bus station ☎ 0256 614 1103 Daily 8.30–5
None
Nyssa (► 51), Alinda (► 40)

Fishing boats moored in the pretty fishing port of Behramkale, below clifftop Assos

AYVALIK

Ottoman Greeks founded Ayvalık in the 16th century and it was soon the most important town on the coast after İzmir, but after the War of Independence the Greek population was sent to Greece in exchange for Muslims from Lesbos and Crete. The town's mosques are mostly Greek Orthodox churches with minarets added on, and a stroll takes you past fine examples of domestic Ottoman architecture. A causeway leads to the island of Alibey, which has fish restaurants, but it is best to go there on one of the boats which regularly depart from the quayside. The dock for boats to and from the Greek island of Lésvos (Lesbos) is close by, a little to the north.The hotels are all in the nearby beach resort of Sarimsaklı.

30A4
About halfway between Çanakkale and İzmir
On quayside 0266 312 2122 May–end Sep daily 9–1, 2–7
Restaurants (£–££)
Dolmuş/minibus from Çanakkale, Assos, Bergama, İzmir
Bergama (➤ 36), Pergamum (➤ 24)

Below: *the Roman Red Basilica in Bergama*

BERGAMA

Bergama covers part of the glorious ancient city of Pergamum: the lofty acropolis rises at one end of the town, and the Asklepeion lies at the other (➤ 24).

Bergama itself is a market town where a donkey and cart is as likely to run you over as one of the tour buses bringing visitors to Pergamum. The archaeological and enthographic museum is not far from the tourist office, and has a very good collection of statuary from Pergamum. The Kızıl Avlu (Red Basilica), at the bottom of the acropolis, was originally a pagan temple, but was converted to a basilica by the Byzantines.

30B4
100km (62 miles) north of İzmir, 50km (31 miles) southeast of Ayvalık
➤ 92 (£-££)
Buses from Ayvalık and İzmir
Atatürk Meydanı
0232 631 2851
Daily 8.30–7, summer; Mon–Fri 8.30–12, 12.30–5.30, winter
Pergamum (➤ 24)

BOZCAADA

According to Homer, the Greeks hid their fleet at Bozcaada while waiting for the Trojans to take the wooden horse in to Troy (➤ 55). The island is only 5km (3 miles) wide, has no resort hotels and some fine beaches along the south coast. Near where boats dock are the ruins of a vast, originally Byzantine, castle (open daily 10–1, 2–7, Apr–Nov). The traditional architecture in the island's only town has been well preserved, and there are several *pansiyons*.

- 30A5
- Just off the coast, south of Troy, 60km (37 miles) southwest of Çanakkale
- Restaurants (£) near quayside
- Ferry from Yükyeri İskelesi (*dolmuş*/minibus from Çanakkale)

ÇANAKKALE

Çanakkale lies between East and West, overlooking the narrow Dardanelles strait (➤ 38), with Gallipoli on the far side and Troy just to the south. The place breathes history and mythology, and this romantic atmosphere is enhanced by the coming and going of boats at the docks. Boats also leave for Gökçeada. The docks are the nucleus of the town, and near them are all the hotels and restaurants and the tourist office. A small bazaar area lies inland between the park and the main dock. The formidable Ottoman castle is now a military museum and there are great views from here. A couple of kilometres out of town on the road to Troy is an archaeological museum with a varied collection of artefacts from the region, including Troy.

- 30A5
- 30km (18 miles) northeast of Troy
- Plenty (£–££)
- Buses from Ayvalık, Istanbul, İzmir, Troy
- By dock ☎ 0286 217 1187
- Gallipoli (➤ 44), Troy (➤ 55), Gökçeada (➤ 45)
- Tours to Gallipoli and Troy

Below: *The seafront in Çanakkale*

30A5
İskele Meydan, 67 Çanakkale 0286 217 1187 Daily 8.30–7, summer; daily 8.30–12.30, 1.30–5.30, winter
Restaurants (£–££) in Çanakkale overlooking Çanakkale Boğazi
Buses from Ayvalık, Istanbul, İzmir, Troy
Gallipoli (➤ 44), Troy (➤ 55), Gökçeada (➤ 45)
Tours to Gallipoli from Çanakkale (➤ 44) start with a ferry journey across the Dardanelles

ÇANAKKALE BOĞAZİ (DARDANELLES)

The sea lane that connects the Aegean with the Sea of Marmara has had strategic significance for thousands of years, and has played a crucial part in history and mythology. It was seen as the dividing line between Asia and Europe when the Persian army under Xerxes crossed it on the way to invade Greece in 480BC, and it is still the dividing line today. In 1915 the British and French fleets tried to push through the Dardanelles and capture Istanbul, but failed disastrously (➤ 44). In Greek mythology, a woman called Helle fell into the water while fleeing from her mother-in-law and drowned—hence the strait's ancient name of 'Hellespont' (Helle's Sea). In another Greek tale, Leander would swim across to meet his lover, Hero, a priestess of Venus, on the European side. When he was drowned one night, the heartbroken Hero drowned herself too. The poet Byron swam across the Hellespont in 1810.

30A4
40km (25 miles) southwest of Bergama
Restaurants and cafes (£–££) along the seafront
Bus from İzmir
Bergama (➤ 36)

ÇANDARLI

This small fishing village emerges from hibernation to become a low-key resort between April and October. Çandarlı, site of ancient Pitane, is a place to relax in, enjoy sea walks along the coarse-sand beach and unhurried meals at one of the seafood restaurants. The atmosphere is laid back, but inviting. A well-preserved 14th-century Genoese castle, although not open to the public, lends character. The liveliest time to visit is on a Friday, when there is a market.

Çandarlı's popular market is in the town square

Çanakkale to Bursa

This is a long drive and you will need to stay overnight in the spa town of Bursa (treatments available). If you want to return to Çanakkale instead, turn back after visiting the Kuşcenneti Milliparkı (National Park).

The E90 connects Çanakkale with Bursa. The first 45km (28 miles) will take you gently up and down hills to beyond the village of Lâpseki (ancient Lampsacus, the traditional birthplace of the phallic god Priapus). There are occasional views of the Dardanelles on the left. Then the road moves inland for about 70km (43 miles), returning to the coast at Denizkent. Some 35km (22 miles) later, you will reach the town of Bandırma.

From Bandırma follow the road to Balıkesir for 13km (8 miles) and look for a sign on the right pointing the 5km (3 miles) to the Kuşcenneti National Park (➤ 49). After visiting the park, return to the main road and turn right back on to the E90. Just under 40km (25 miles) before Bursa, look for a sign pointing right for the fishing village of Gölyazı, 6km (4 miles) from the main road.

Gölyazı is situated by the side of a lake, Uluabat Gölü, and is built over the ruins of ancient Apollonia. Ancient city walls and a large deserted Greek church are the main points of interest besides the pleasant scenes of everyday life in a Turkish fishing village.

Return to the main road and complete the journey to Bursa.

Park near the tourist office, in the town centre, and collect a town map and brochure before going to explore the Ottoman houses and other monuments of the city.

Distance
340km (211 miles)
(200km (124 miles) to/from Kuşcenneti National Park)

Time
8–10 hours

Start point
Çanakkale
30A5

End point
Bursa
30C5

Lunch
Appolonia Restaurant (£)
North end of the village of Gölyazı

Ottoman architecture in Bursa

ÇEŞME (► 18, TOP TEN)

- 30A4
- Gülpinar, 20km (12.5 miles) west of Assos
- Restaurants (£) in Babakale
- Occasional *dolmuş*/minibus from Assos
- None
- Free
- Assos (► 34)

CHRYSE

All that remains of Chryse is the ruined temple of Apollo Smintheon, signposted in the village of Gülpinar, but it is a place of significance in Homer's account of the Trojan War. It was from here that the Greek leader Agamemnon took Chryseis, the daughter of the priest of Apollo, for a mistress. He later grudgingly returned her, to appease Apollo, but only after demanding the mistress of Achilles as compensation and causing a major row in the process. This is the place to read Book I of the *Iliad*, and the landscape makes the journey from Assos very pleasant. The road continues west to Babakale, passing a turning on the way to a lovely beach at Akliman.

- 30B2
- 28km (17 miles) south of Kuşadası
- 0256 646 1079
- Daily 9–8
- Snack bars on beaches
- *Dolmuş*/minibus from Kuşadası
- None Inexpensive
- Kuşadası (► 46–47), Priene (► 52)

DİLEK MİLLİPARKI

This national park covers a large area of mountains, marsh and beaches, but some parts are used by the military and access to these is strictly prohibited. What remains open, however, is amply rewarding for anyone seeking fresh air and a break from ancient temples or busy resorts. From the park's entrance it is about 10km to the last of the pebbly but pretty beaches along the way. The last beach, Karasu, makes a particularly pleasant spot for a picnic. In the higher areas, you should see birds of prey. The marshes have waterbirds.

*The Lanner falcon (*Falco biarmicus*) may be seen in Dilek Milliparkı*

- 30B4
- 120km (75 miles) south of Çanakkale
- Local food (£) served in Ören's market; hotel restaurants
- *Dolmuş*/minibus from Çanakkale and Ayvalik
- Assos (► 34), Ayvalık (► 36)

EDREMİT AND ÖREN

There is little to interest the tourist in Edremit, but visitors travelling by public transport along the north Aegean coast are likely to find themselves waiting for a *dolmuş*/minibus connection here. The village of Burhaniye is about 15km to the south and a *dolmuş*/minibus from here goes to the pretty, low-key resort of Ören, 4km away. There is a splendid beach, and the coastal road heading west towards Küçükukuyu is lined with moderately priced hotels and *pansiyons*.

Around Efes (Ephesus)

From the ticket office walk straight ahead to the marble-paved path.

The theatre is on the left, and on the right is the Arcadian Way, one of the few streets outside Rome to have street-lighting in ancient times.

Go to the theatre (► 19) and climb the steps. You can go straight to the theatre's seating area, or turn right near the top of the steps by the solitary tree, and enter the theatre orchestra through the roofed passageway. Leave the theatre on the opposite side.

About halfway along the marble-paved street, look for the brothel sign (a footprint and a female face) etched on a pavement stone on the right side, protected by a metal frame.

At the end of this street, the two-storey façade of the Celsus Library (► 42–43) is on the right. Turn left, up a gradually sloping marble-paved street.

Look for the Roman public toilets on the left and the ancient spice shop. Next comes Hadrian's Temple. Inside the temple entrance, on the right side, note the 13 carved figures on the walls: Athena and other deities alongside a Roman family. The originals and an explanation are in the Ephesus Museum in Selçuk (► 53).

Carry on up the street until a sign points right to the museum of inscriptions.

The delightful odeon (theatre) up on the left makes an ideal picnic stop. You can leave from the Upper Entrance, just ahead, or retrace your route to the Lower Entrance.

Distance
2km/1 mile (4km/2.5 miles if returning to start point)

Time
3–4 hours

Start point
Lower Entrance
30B3

End point
Upper Entrance/
Lower Entrance
30B3

Lunch
The restaurants at the Lower Entrance are not recommended. Bring a picnic and, on a hot day, plenty of water. Restaurants in Selçuk

This temple at Ephesus is dedicated to the emperor Hadrian

- 30B3
- 3km (2 miles) from Selçuk tourist office
- 0232 892 6402/6940
- Daily 8–6.30, summer; daily 8–5.30, winter
- Restaurants (not recommended) at the Lower Entrance. Bring a picnic or eat in Selçuk (£–££)
- Buses to Selçuk from Kuşadası and İzmir

EFES (EPHESUS)

Ephesus was the capital of the Roman province of Asia Minor. It was a major political and cultural centre, and the Romans spared no expense in making this a showcase city for their civilization. It has been very well preserved and is one of the major ancient sites around the Mediterranean. Long before the Romans, Ephesus was home to the cult of Cybele, a mother-goddess. Cybele merged easily with the Greek goddess Artemis, worshipped by the Athenian colonizers who founded a settlement here around 1000BC. Ephesus flourished under Rome and was abandoned only in the sixth century AD after the harbour had silted up.

At least half a day is needed to explore the city (see the Efes walk, ➤ 41). You can join a guided tour, although a guide is not essential because the site is compact and there are many specialist guidebooks at the entrance, in the Selçuk tourist office or in the bookshop across the road from it. The highlights include the theatre (➤ 19) and the Library of Celsus.

The scant remains of the temple of Artemis, one of the Seven Wonders of the Ancient World, are passed on the walk from Selçuk to the entrance (signposted as the Artemision, on the left side of the road).

The Library of Celsus, built between AD110 and

Did you know ?

*When Mark Twain visited Ephesus he found 'exquisitely sculptured marble fragments scattered thick among the dust and weeds' (*The Innocents Abroad, *1869). H V Morton made a visit in 1936, and noted 'no sign of life but a goat herd leaning on a broken sarcophagus or a lonely peasant outlined against a mournful sunset. Few people ever visit it'. This is a far cry from the scene today but, out of season, it is still possible to wander through the city virtually alone.*

135, is an impressive and beautiful structure. The four niches on the two-storeyed façade are filled with plaster copies of the statues of the Four Virtues—Goodness, Thought, Knowledge and Wisdom—whose originals now reside in Vienna.

Beyond the three-arched gateway on the north (right) side is the main *agora* (marketplace—note that it may be off-limits to visitors). Graffiti, both ancient and modern, adorns the walls of the gateway. One inscription in Greek praises the work of a food inspector in fixing the price of bread sold in the agora. The library could hold some 14,000 book scrolls. Peer through the grill in the front right corner to see the metre-wide cavity that protected them from winter damp.

The marbled street that runs uphill from the Library of Celsus (➤ 41) has been completely restored on one side, showing the toilets, baths, shops, homes and a temple as they once were. The other side of the street is still the subject of prolonged restoration work by an Austrian archaeological project. At the top of the marbled street, one relief is all that remains of the Gate of Hercules. Here the road branches to the right for the Temple to Domitian, one of Rome's more insane emperors (AD 81–96). The left route leads past a temple, and on to an odeon, a 1,400-seat theatre, which has been restored. If you are in need of a shady corner, the theatre serves well as a picnic site.

In Selçuk ☎ (0232) 892 1328
None
Moderate
Selçuk (➤ 53), Meryemana (➤ 50), Kuşadası (➤ 46–47), Magnesia on the Maeander (➤ 49)
Regular tours from most resorts

Below: *Looking up at the meticulously restored façade of the Library of Celsus (bottom)*

FOÇA

30A3
70km (43 miles) northwest of İzmir
Restaurants (£–££)
Atatürk Bulvarı, just north of central square
0232 812 5534
Bus from İzmir
Çandarlı (➤ 38), İzmir (➤ 31)

Nowadays a summer haunt of İzmir's well-to-do, the twin villages of Eski Foça and Yeni Foça (Old and New) were founded in ancient times by Greek colonists who called their colony Phocaea. The Phoceans were famed seafarers, and are credited with founding Massilia (Marseilles). Apart from a fourth century BC tomb, Taş Kule, there is precious little left of the ancient city, but it is a pretty place with some fish restaurants.

GELİBOLU (GALLIPOLI)

30A5
35-km (22-mile) long peninsula opposite Çanakkale
Sites are open 24 hours;
Restaurants (£–££) in Gelibolu
Passenger and vehicle ferry from Çanakkale, or join a tour
None
Çanakkale (➤ 37), Troy (➤ 55)
Tours available

Military Museum
0283 814 1297
Inexpensive
Daily 8.30–5.30; closes 12–1 in winter

Gelibolu, a pretty town on the narrow peninsula of land opposite Çanakkale Boğazı (Dardanelles) synonymous with a momentous battle of World War I. When the French and British fleets failed to force their way through the Dardanelles (➤ 38), Winston Churchill ordered a troop landing to knock out the Turkish troops guarding the strait. The aim was to secure the Dardanelles, take Istanbul, and organize logistical support for their Russian allies through the Black Sea, but the plan failed in the face of furious Turkish resistance. Thousands of Allied soldiers were killed and over 55,000 Turks lost their lives in one of the worst battles of the war. There are organized tours of the battlefield sites and memorials from Çanakkale. One well-established tour company is Hassle Free Travel Agency (tel: 0286 213 5969; www.anzachouse.com). Start at the Kabatepe Military Museum in the centre of the peninsula (open daily 8–12, 1–5) and pick up a leaflet that will guide you around the various landing beaches, memorials and cemeteries. Allow plenty of time. You will need your own transport if you do not join an organized tour, because the sites are spread out across a wide area.

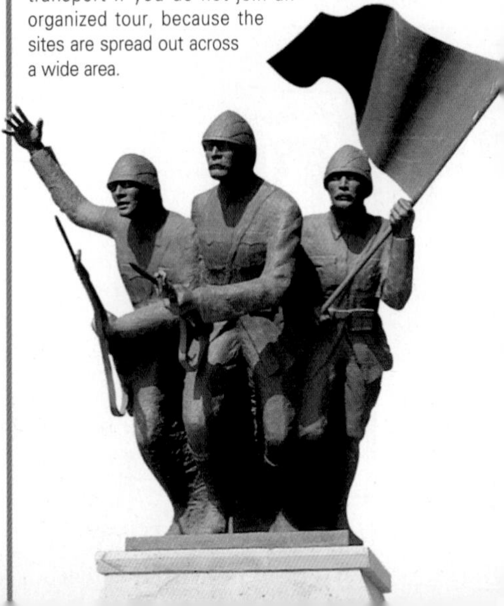

The war memorial on the Gelibolu (Gallipoli) peninsula

GÖKÇEADA

The larger of Turkey's two islands close to Çanakkale Boğazı (Dardanelles) in the North Aegean (the other is Bozcaada, ➤ 37), Gökçeada has the open prison from which William Hayes, of *Midnight Express* fame, escaped. You will need your own transport to reach the island's small villages. There is a pleasant beach on the north coast at Kaleköy, which can also be reached by *dolmuş*.

- 30A5
- 30km (19 miles) west of Çanakkale
- Fish restaurants (£)
- Ferry from Çanakkale
- Çanakkale (➤ 37), Troy (➤ 55), Çanakkale Boğazı (➤ 38), Gelibolu (Gallipoli, ➤ 44)

HERAKLEIA

Originally part of the ancient kingdom of Caria, Herakleia was fortified and Hellenized in the fourth century BC. The signposted sites are spread out, around and in the small village of Kapıkırı. A good place to start is at the sanctuary of Endymion (see below). As you walk towards the road from the sanctuary, a sign points to Carian rock tombs on the right. To see them, clamber over the wall and head for the remains of a Byzantine castle on the headland. From the rocks on the other side of the castle walls you can look down on the Carian coffins cut out of the rock.

- 30B2
- In village of Kapıkırı
- Open access at all times
- Restaurants (£)
- *Dolmuş*/minibus from Çamiçi or by boat across Lake Bafa
- None
- Free
- Euromos (➤ 68), Labranda (➤ 77), Milas (➤ 83), Drive from Kuşadası (➤ 48)

HIERAPOLIS (➤ 20, TOP TEN)

Did you know ?

According to tradition, Zeus granted Endymion his wish for eternal youth by sending him to sleep and to dream for ever on Mount Latmos. The moon goddess, Selene, fell in love with him and bore him 50 daughters while he slept.

Above: *The modern village of Kapıkırı has developed next to the ruins of ancient Herakleia*

KUŞADASI ✪✪

30B3

95km (59 miles) south of İzmir, 20km (12.5 miles) south of Ephesus

Restaurants (£–£££)

Dolmuş/minibus from Bodrum, İzmir, Pamukkale, Selçuk, Söke

Liman Caddesi
0256 614 1103; fax 0256 614 6295; www.kusadasi.com; www.merhotels.com
Daily 8–5.30, summer (8–8 Jul–Aug); Mon–Fri 8–12, 1–5, winter

Ephesus (➤ 19 and 41–43), Selçuk (➤ 53), Meryemana (➤ 50), Miletos (➤ 50), Didyma (➤ 66), Priene (➤ 52), Magnesia on the Maeander (➤ 49), Notion and Klaros (➤ 51)

This is one of the major resorts on the Aegean coast and unashamedly proclaimed as such by the scores of carpet shops, jewellers and leatherware stores that fill the town centre. The large harbour, which in summer receives half a dozen cruise ships each day, faces Samos, and the 2km (1-mile) trip to the Greek island is a popular diversion for people staying in Kuşadası. Kuşadası offers a wide range of entertainment in addition to shopping. At night the pubs, discos (➤ 112–113),Turkish baths (➤ 115) and restaurants (➤ 94–5) are bursting at the seams with happy holidaymakers determined to have a good time. During the day, water-based activities are very popular, and most of the big hotels are able to offer a wide range of sports.

Kuşadası is so dedicated to hedonism that the lack of places of interest within the town itself hardly matters; the most interesting site is the small Bird Island, connected to the mainland by a 400m (437 yards) causeway and home to a 16th-century Genoese fortress, which now houses a number of cafés. Kuşadası is well placed, however, for visits to many of the Turkish Aegean's most extraordinary ancient sites. Ephesus is a short bus ride away, and the ancient Greek settlements of Milet (Miletus), Didim (Didyma) and Priene may be easily visited by public transport or on a three-in-a-day guided tour. Aphrodisias, Pamukkale and Hierapolis are a couple of hours away by road.

The main esplanade, Atatürk Bulvarı, runs past the harbour where boats to and from Samos dock. The nearby Öküz Mehmet Pasa

The Genoese castle on Bird Island is alive with cafés and nightclubs

Kervansaray (now a noisy hotel) is a useful landmark in this town, which has no obvious centre. At the junction of the hotel and the esplanade, a pedestrianized street, Barbaros Hayrettin Bulvarı, runs inland. To the left, as you ascend this street, lies the old part of town, known as Kale, where some picturesque buildings have been converted into clubs, bars and restaurants.

Kadinlar Plaji (Ladies' Beach), 3km (2 miles) southwest of town and easily reached by minibus, has a cluster of resort hotels and is very well known, but the cleaner pools of nearby hotels may seem more inviting. A better choice is Tusan beach, 5km (3 miles) from the other side of town on the road to Selçuk and also easily reached by minibus.

Moderately priced accommodation is available near the town centre; the 4- and 5-star hotels are stretched out in bunches along the coastline at either end of town, but they are nearly all easily reached by minibuses from the seafront road. These minibuses will usually stop opposite the main bus station, which is outside town on the main İzmir–Söke road. This can be an uncomfortably long walk in summer, but to get to Söke (the major local transport hub and the departure point for buses to places of historical interest) there is an unofficial minibus meeting point nearer to the centre of town, and most of the hotel minibuses also stop here.

Ladies' Beach welcomes both sexes throughout the year

Ancient Caria

Distance
178km (110 miles)

Time
4–6 hours, depending of length of stops

Start/end point
Kuşadası
30B3

Lunch
Zeybek or Agora restaurant (£)

This drive leaves from the hustle and bustle of Kuşadası to explore the ancient kingdom of Caria, taking in Lake Bafa and a number of interesting Hellenic sites, some of which are difficult to reach without your own transport.

From Kuşadası take the road to Söke (515) and when it meets the main İzmir–Milas road, the 525, turn right, signposted for Milas, and head south. Once the road starts to hug the shores of Lake Bafa park by one of the lake-side restaurants.

It is possible to take a swim in the lake, and there are passenger boats to Herakleıa (➤ 45). This drive, however, takes you to Herakleıa by road.

Bafa Gölü (Lake Bafa) with ancient Herakleıa on the far side

Drive on about 6km to the village of Çamiçi and take the road signposted left to Herakleıa. After visiting Herakleıa, return to Çamiçi and turn left to continue towards Milas for about 15km (9 miles). Look for a signpost on the left to Euromos (➤ 68), 1km south of the village of Selimiye.

After visiting Euromos, continue for another 12km (7.5 miles) and turn left at the sign for Kargicak if you wish to make the 14km (9 miles) detour to Labranda (➤ 77). The road is narrow, with tarmac washed away on both sides and plenty of low gear shifting will be needed to make the steep ascent.

Return to the main road. If time permits, it is only a few kilometres further on to Milas (➤ 83). Otherwise, turn right when meeting the main road from Kargicak and return to Kuşadası.

KUŞCENNETİ MİLLİPARKI (NATIONAL PARK)

This bird sanctuary, whose name translates as 'Bird Paradise', lies between Çanakkale and Bursa (➤ 39). An exhibit inside the entrance shows what birds may be seen from the nearby observation post (bring your own binoculars). Herons, cormorants, pelicans and spoonbills frequent the reserve and you may see the occasional spotted eagle. Between April and June and September to November are the best times to visit because so many species migrate at these times. Over 250 species have been identified.

- 30B5
- 20km (12.5 miles) south of Bandırma
- Daily 7–5.30
- Bus from Çanakkale
- None
- Inexpensive

*Spoonbills (*Platalea leucorodia*) grace Kuşcenneti National Park*

LAODIKEIÁ (LAODICEIA)

Ancient Laodiceia was founded in the third century BC and flourished until an earthquake in the fifth century AD. The city inspired St. John the Divine's acerbic comment on a civilian population that failed to embrace Christianity as quickly as he anticipated: 'I know your works, you are neither hot nor cold... So because you are lukewarm, and neither hot nor cold, I will spew you out of my mouth.' The Roman ruins include a gymnasium and baths, two theatres and the remnants of a stadium. There is no public transport to the site; you can get a taxi in Pamukkale, but it is best to drive yourself.

- 30C3
- 14km (9 miles) south of Pamukkale, 5km (3 miles) north of Denizli
- Open 24 hours
- Taxi from Pamukkale
- None
- Free
- Pamukkale (➤ 22–23), Hierapolis (➤ 20), Afrodisias (➤ 34)

MAGNESIA ON THE MAEANDER

Homesick colonists from Magnesia in Greece founded this ancient city and it was presented to the Athenian Themistocles by a Persian king. He is said to have committed suicide here while making a sacrifice at the Temple of Artemis. It requires some imagination to make sense of the scattered remains of this temple but it is likely you'll have the place to yourself, which gives it a certain charm.

- 30B3
- 16km (10 miles) north of Söke
- Daily 8.30–dusk
- *Dolmuş*/minibus from Söke or Selçuk
- Inexpensive
- Ephesus (➤ 42–43), Meryemana (➤ 50), Kuşadası (➤ 46)

30B3
40km (25 miles) northeast of İzmir
Restaurants (£)
Buses from İzmir, Sart or Salihli; train from İzmir
Anafartalar Mah 1 MKP Cad 0236 232 3347
Mon–Sat 8–12, 1–5
Sardis (➤ 53), İzmir (➤ 31)

MANİSA

Founded in the aftermath of the fall of Troy and destroyed by Greeks soldiers retreating in 1922 (➤ 10–11), contemporary Manisa is a modern town with a commercial air, redeemed by a grand backdrop of mountains and a city centre worth a half day's exploration. The tourist office is in the centre of town and you can pick up a map and brochure there before setting out to visit the three 16th-century mosques and a small museum with material from Sart (Sardis, ➤ 53).

30B3
8km (5 miles) south of Ephesus
0232 892 6094
Dawn–dusk
Café (£) near entrance
Taxi from Selçuk
Inexpensive
Ephesus (➤ 41–43), Selçuk (➤ 53)

MERYEMANA

The story that the Virgin Mary came to Ephesus with St Paul gained credibility in the early 19th century, when a German nun who had never been to Turkey described a vision of the house where Mary stayed. A priest in İzmir matched the description with a chapel just south of Ephesus. Sanctioned by a papal visit in 1967, Meryemana is now regarded as the place where Mary lived out her last years, and receives a steady stream of pilgrims.

30B2
22km (14 mjiles) south of Priene
0256 875 5401
Daily 8–5
Overpriced snack bars near the entrance

MİLET (MILETOS)

By far the most important of the Greek colonies established along the Aegean coast, Miletos was originally on an inlet of the sea, but a marshy delta, much loved by frogs, has now formed around the site. The remains you see today belong to the city re-created after a destructive onslaught by the Persians in 495BC. When a play on the

Seats in the theatre of Miletos, and a detail from a fallen column

Persian defeat of Miletos was performed in ancient Athens the audience burst into tears and the playwright was fined for causing such dismay. The large theatre is a good vantage point to view the site, which was laid out in a grid pattern (still visible). Parts of a *nymphaeum* (fountain), *agora* (market-place), and Roman baths survive.

- *Dolmuş*/minibus from Söke
- None
- Inexpensive
- Priene (➤ 52), Didyma (➤ 66)
- Tours from Kuşadası combine Miletos, Priene and Didyma

NOTİON AND KLAROS ✪

Notion was a typically small ancient Greek settlement, and although very little remains today, the site is attractively located and offers a fine view of the sea. Signposts lead from Notion to the site of ancient Klaros just over 1km away. Never a city, Klaros was famed for its temple and oracle of Apollo (presently undergoing excavation and restoration), whose priest was able to answer the needs of those making a consultation without ever hearing their question. The source of inspiration was a sacred spring and parts of the underground chamber enclosing it can be clearly made out.

- 30B3
- 25km (22 miles) north of Kuşadası
- Dawn–dusk
- *Dolmuş*/minibus from Kuşadası to Seferihisar. Ask for Notion
- None
- Free
- Kuşadası (➤ 46–47), Ephesus (➤ 41–43), Selçuk (➤ 53)

NYSSA ✪

Many of Turkey's minor ancient Greek and Roman sites have attractive settings, and Nyssa's is especially so. The city was founded in the third century BC and flourished well into Roman times. Strabo, a geographer of the first century BC, described it as a 'double city', and there are some remains of two bridges that linked the settlement across a tumultuous stream. A theatre and semi-circular *bouleuterion* (meeting hall) are the main sights; the long tunnel that the citizens built to help drain the city can also be made out. Nyssa is not visited by tour buses but it is easy to reach by car or public transport and, like Notion and Klaros (➤ above), makes a good day trip from Kuşadası.

- 30B3
- 2km from Sultanhisar, 14km west of Nazilli
- Daily 8.30–dusk
- Restaurants (£) in Sultanhisar
- Buses between Kuşadası and Denizli will stop at Sultanhisar
- None
- Inexpensive
- Aydın (➤ 35)

PAMUKKALE (➤ 21–22, TOP TEN)

PERGAMUM (➤ 24, TOP TEN)

- 30B2
- 35km (22 miles) south of Kuşadası
- 0256 547 1165
- Daily 8.30–sunset
- Restaurants (£) in adjoining village of Güllübahçe
- *Dolmuş*/minibus from Söke
- None
- Inexpensive
- Kuşadası (➤ 46–47), Ephesus (➤ 19 and 41–43), Selçuk (➤ 53), Meryemana (➤ 50), Miletos (➤ 50), Didyma (➤ 66), Magnesia on the Maeander (➤ 49)
- Tours from Kuşadası combine Priene, Miletos and Didyma

Above: *The ancient city of Priene makes an enjoyable day's excursion from Kuşadası*

PRIENE

Ancient Priene, founded around the 11th century BC, now lies under the alluvial plain, but the city that developed from the fourth century BC high on the mountain above is in remarkably good shape. It never attracted much attention from the Romans, and the happy result is a Hellenistic city uncluttered by Roman or Byzantine additions and modifications. The theatre should not be missed: the front row has five marble thrones for special guests, and faces the altar of Dionysus, where a sacrifice began the day's entertainment. The two-storey stage and its projecting proscenium have, to a remarkable degree, weathered the last 2,000 years, and the holes and sockets for decorated wooden panels may be seen clearly on some of the front pillars which held up the stage.

The Temple of Athena Polias was regarded in ancient times as the epitome of Ionic temple architecture. When English archaeologists arrived in the 1860s the temple walls were still standing at over 1.5m (5ft) in places. To the north of the temple lie the scant remains of a sanctuary to Demeter and Kore; far more substantial are the remains of the *bouleuterion* (meeting hall) to the south of the theatre. The gymnasium and small stadium, on the south, lower front side of the site, are worth seeking out. Some of the starting blocks for foot races can still be made out. It's a steep walk up to the site from the car park, but the setting is truly stunning. Remember to take water.

SART (SARDIS)

There are two main sites at Sart: the Greek Temple of Artemis and the Roman city of the fifth century AD. The wonderful Temple of Artemis is signposted on the right, as you come from İzmir, and is reached after a 1km (half a mile) walk. The setting is idyllic, surrounded by pinnacles of rock, with the occasional tinkling of sheep bells in the background as a shepherd moves his flock. Although only two columns remain completely upright, there is plenty to inspire the imagination. An Ionic capital, resting in front of a rusting excavators crane, is reputed to be one of the best examples you are likely see at such close quarters. The Roman town has been excavated and restored.

- 30B3
- 100km east of İzmir
- Daily 8–6, closes for lunch in winter
- Two köfte restaurants in Salihli (9km/5.5 miles)
- Bus from İzmir
- None | Inexpensive

A visit to the Ephesus Museum in Selçuk complements a day among the ruins

SELÇUK

The tourist industry in this small town is entirely due to its proximity to Ephesus. It makes an ideal place for a short stay because it is also close to the ancient sites south of Kuşadası. The Ephesus Museum displays finds from Ephesus: do not miss the Artemis Room, with its many-breasted statue of the goddess. The adjoining ethnographic section is also recommended. The Hill of Ayasoluk towers over the town, with Byzantine-Turkish fortifications and the remains of St. John's Basilica, built to mark the final resting place of St. John the Evangelist. From Selçuk you can make a pleasant day trip to the old Greek town of Sirince, only 8km (5 miles) away.

- 30B3
- 20km (12.5 miles) northeast of Kuşadası
- Restaurants (£–££)
- Bus from İzmir, *dolmuş*/ minibus from Kuşadası
- Atatürk Mah 0232 892 6328; www.selcuk.gov.tr Mon–Fri 8.30–5.30, Sat, Sun 9–5 in summer
- Kuşadası (➤ 46–47), Ephesus (➤ 19 and 41–43)

SİĞACIK AND TEOS

- 30A3
- 40km (25 miles) southwest of İzmir
- Open 24 hours
- Restaurants (£) in Siğacık
- *Dolmuş*/minibus from İzmir
- None
- Free
- İzmir (➤ 31), Çeşme (➤ 18)

A tiny harbour and the remains of a Genoese fortress dominate the fishing village of Siğacık

The lack of a sandy beach ensures that Siğacık, a village that has grown up inside the walls of a Genoese fortress, remains a low-key destination. Just 1.5km (1 mile) away, however, the beach at Akkum is a developing resort that is steadily and relentlessly encroaching on Siğacık. The site of ancient Teos, 5km from Siğacık, is the best reason for visiting this stretch of coastline between İzmir and Çeşme. Travel author Freya Stark wrote: 'It is where I should live, if I had the choice of all the cities of Ionia.' The city was the birthplace of the lyric poet Anakreon (*c* 540BC) and was a renowned centre for the cult of Dionysus, a Greek nature god of vegetation and fruitfulness, particularly associated with wine and ecstacy. The remains of a Temple of Dionysus, once the largest in the ancient world, are the ruined site's main attraction.

TRUVA (TROY) ✪✪

Troy was thought to have existed only in Homer's imagination until excavations began in 1870, financed by the German businessman Heinrich Schliemann, who was obsessed with finding the historical city. He discovered not one but four settlements, built over the ruins of each other, and later excavations suggest that there were nine main periods of occupation. The first five, known as Troy I to Troy V (3000–1800BC), follow a similar cultural pattern, but a change then occurs, as prosperity grew from maritime trading links in the Aegean and the Black Sea. This could have brought conflict with the Greeks, who besiege Troy in Homer's *Iliad.* The epic poem tells a highly charged tale of war, love and honour, aided and hindered by the pantheon of Greek gods. It was enormously influential not only for the ancient Greeks, but for later European civilization itself.

Homer's Troy may have been Troy VI (1800–1275BC), which was destroyed either by an earthquake in 1275BC or by being stormed and set on fire (or both, over time). Settlements of the site went on into Roman times, with Troy IX (300 BC–AD300) completing the saga. The enormous wooden horse at the entrance to Troy leaves no doubt as to which of the city's many eras captures the interest of modern visitors.

There is a lot to see, but it is a place of ditches, mounds and fragments rather than great structures. The whole site is surprisingly small, or perhaps only the crowds make it seem so; it is worth turning up early in the morning or as late as possible. When viewed from the city walls, the dismally flat plain that stretches ahead can be evocative of ancient battles and, with only a little imagination, the 300-m (327-ft) stretch of inward-leaning and curving wall of Troy VI will conjure up images of the scene of Hector being dragged by furious Achilles around the city walls. Inside the city one of the most impressive sights is the massive stone ramp that could have carried the Wooden Horse—except that it belongs to Troy II (2500–2300BC).

30A5
25km (15.5 miles) south of Çanakkale
0286 283 0061
Daily 8.30–sunset
Dolmuş/minibus from Çanakkale
None | Inexpensive
Çanakkale (➤ 37), Çanakkale Boğazı (➤ 38), Gallipoli (➤ 44)
Tours from Çanakkale often include Gallipoli (➤ 37)

A replica wooden horse greets you at Troy

Did you know ?

The Trojan treasures that Schliemann took back to Berlin were lost without trace after the Russians took the city in May 1945. They reappeared at an exhibition in Moscow in 1993.

Southern Aegean

Turkey's southern Aegean coast has experienced tourism on a large scale for far longer than the north. Nevertheless, the chief resort town of Bodrum has retained a surprising charm, and it remains one of the most pleasant destinations along the self-styled 'Turkish Riviera'. Its competitor, Marmaris is a little further south and provides easy access to the Greek island of Ródos (Rhodes). At Marmaris the coast begins to turn west, and is known as the 'Turquoise Coast' because of the opaque sky-blue and green-blue colours of the Mediterranean. The small town of Fethiye is an attractive base for a sun, sea and sand holiday, but it is also within easy reach of several fascinating historical sites, dating back to the ancient kingdom of Lycia that once included this corner of the coast.

'The life loving and prosperous people of Physcus [ancient Marmaris] *are blessed with the world's most beautiful rainbow by day, and at night a moon that hangs over the sea like a ball of fire.'*

HERODOTUS, *The Histories*
Fifth century BC

Open-air restaurants beneath Bodrum Castle

Bariş Meydanı 48
☎ 0252 316 1091
Daily 8.30–7, summer; Mon–Fri 8.30–noon, 1–5.30, winter

Buses from Fethiye, İzmir, Kuşadası, Marmaris, Pamukkale

Milas (➤ 83), Turgutreis (➤ 89)

Bodrum

Contemporary Bodrum is a major resort, but still has a traditional Mediterranean flavour, with whitewashed, flat-roofed homes dotting the terraced hillsides. The opening of an international airport, 40km (25 miles) away has given a fresh boost to its thriving tourist industry, and despite lacking its own beach, Bodrum is the most chic and European resort on Turkey's Aegean coast.

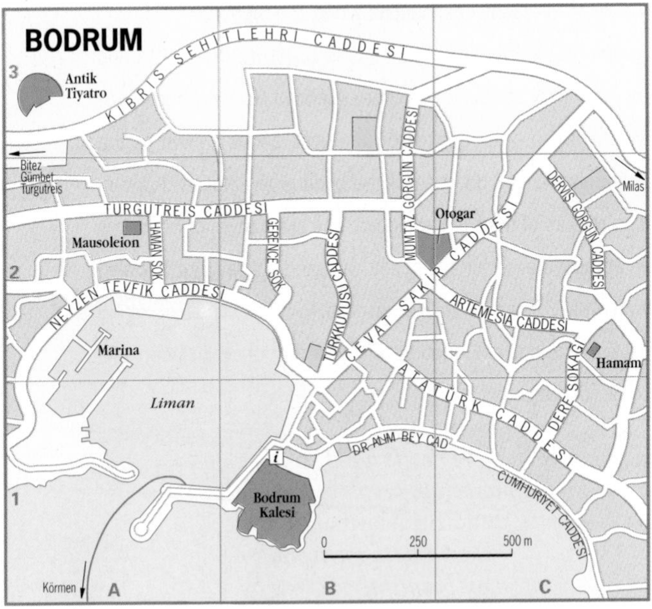

The original name of Bodrum was Halicarnassos and it was founded in the 11th century BC by Greek colonists. Notable inhabitants have included the historian Herodotus (fifth century BC), and Mausolus (377–353BC), who was installed as king after a Persian invasion. Halicarnassos fell into obscurity during Roman and Byzantine times until the Knights of St. John arrived from nearby Rhodes in 1402 and built the massive Castle of St Peter that continues to tower over the town. The word *bodrum* means 'dungeon' or 'underground vault' in Turkish, so its modern name presumably comes from the castle or the Mausoleum.

The medieval Castle of St. Peter stands guard over modern Bodrum

The Castle of St. Peter is the obvious landmark and directly in front of it, due north, is the tourist office. The pedestrianized streets to the north of the tourist office make up the town's bazaar and this is the central shopping area for leather, clothes, carpets and assorted souvenirs and gifts. Dr Alim Bey Caddesi is the main street facing the sea to the east. At the end of the bazaar area the street becomes Cumhuriyet Caddesi, and forms the heart of Bodrum's legendary nightlife. The sea-facing street that follows the harbour's curve to the west of the tourist office, Nezen Tevfik Caddesi, brings you past open-air restaurants and cafés to the marina and the quieter end of town. The main street from the bus station, Cevat İşakir Caddesi, has more shops, restaurants, and the post office.

During the high season Bodrum is definitely not a place for anyone seeking a quiet retreat; the sophisticated night-clubs are the loudest on the coast. The mornings in Bodrum are relatively quiet, but only because so many visitors are sound asleep after carousing and dancing until dawn. The town itself is not overdeveloped, but it acts as a hub for the stream of resorts around the Bodrum peninsula (➤ 62), ensuring the streets are jammed packed.

Bodrum's marina is a favourite destination for yachts cruising the Aegean and Mediterranean, and the town is an ideal place to organize a sailing excursion. Yachts and boats can be hired with or without a crew, and there is no problem finding an agent who will arrange a day trip for those with no experience of sailing. Excursions off the peninsula by road, on the other hand, begin with an hour-long drive to the main coast road. If you are touring, a two-night stay should be sufficient, although the peninsula has plenty to offer by way of sandy beaches, accommodation and restaurants for a lazy couple of weeks.

Bodrum

Distance
5km (3 miles)

Time
2–3 hours

Start point
Tourist office
58B1

End point
Marina
58A2

Lunch
At one of the many seafront restaurants

For general tourist shopping Bodrum has a good variety of merchandise

Walk from the tourist office with the sea on your left until you reach a Y-junction after a few hundred metres/yards. Bear right, passing the minaret of a mosque on the right, and walk up Cevat Sakir Caddesi. Walk past the post office on the left and then turn left, immediately before the otogar *(bus station), on to Mumtaz Gorgün Caddesi. Turn left at the next set of traffic lights and walk down Kulcu Sokak.*

The Picante Restaurant (► 97) is on the left, and although you will be turning left at the next junction, the Epsilon restaurant (► 96) is reached by going straight ahead at the junction and looking for an alleyway on the right.

Turn left at the junction past the Picante restaurant into Turkkuyusu Caddesi. This street is full of small shops, hairdressers and signposts pointing the way to inexpensive accommodatino. At the end of the street you reach the mosque passed earlier. Turn right for a walk by the water's edge along Neyzen Tevfik Caddesi to the marina.

There are lots of restaurants facing the sea here, take time to read the menus and find the nationality of your choice.

What to See in Bodrum

BEACHES

The nearest beach on the Bodrum peninsula itself is Gümbet, 3km (2 miles) away and easily reached by *dolmuş*, or on foot when the temperature drops (take the road inland after passing the marina). Gümbet, overdeveloped with package hotels, is the preserve of 18- to 30-year-olds. Further west is a mediocre beach at the more upmarket Bitez, and a better one at Ortakent (which is popular with Turkish families on holiday).

Kagı, Bağla, Karaincir and Akyarlar, on the south coast of the peninsula, are quieter locations but have watersports (equipment for hire), and the sea is cleaner here than it is at the beaches nearer Bodrum.

30B2
Restaurants and beach cafés (£–££)
Dolmuş/minibus/boat from Bodrum
Turgutreis (► 89), Gümbet (► 72), Yalıkavak (► 90)

Did you know ?

Bodrum has a reputation as the capital of cosmopolitan nightlife on the Aegean coast. The spectacular open-air Disco Halikarnas on Cumhuriyet Caddesi (► 114), accommodates over 2,000 stomping dancers until the sun begins to rise over the harbour, and there are scores of smaller but equally lively discos and bars.

BODRUM KALESI (CASTLE OF ST. PETER ► 17, TOP TEN)

GÖKOVA KÖRFEZI (GULF OF GÖKOVA)

There are boats and yachts for hire and agents to arrange day trips along Dr Alim Bey Caddesi near the tourist office, and at the main marina, off Neyzen Tevfik Caddesi. A typical itinerary visits the island of Karaada, which has hot springs and mud baths, before continuing to Ortakent beach (► 84) and skirting the Greek island of Kos for a swim and lunch. Boats returning to Bodrum often pause at a shallow stretch of water christened 'the Aquarium' because of the marine life that can be seen.

30B2
See also separate entry for Gököva Korfesi (► 72)

Snorkelling is one of the most enjoyable and easy-to-organize watersports along the Aegean coast

58A2
Turgutreis Caddesi
Daily 8–5
None nearby
None
Inexpensive

Above: *jet skis can be hired from the beaches around Bodrum*

MAUSOLEION (MAUSOLEUM)

Mausolus ruled ancient Caria for the Persians as a semi-independent state, and his love of Greek culture reached its zenith in the splendid tomb—the first 'mausoleum'—erected after his death in 351BC. It was one of the Seven Wonders of the Ancient World, but the Knights of St. John demolished it for materials for their castle. The massive foundations remain, but little else—assorted column pieces, parts of the outer wall and underground vault. The site is still worth a visit, as an informative exhibition with models gives some flesh to the meagre remains. There are also plaster copies and a few original pieces of the so-called Amazon reliefs that were mostly shipped off to join other hijacked treasures in the British Museum in London.

58A3
Dolmuş/minibus

TIYATRO (THEATRE)

To the northwest of the mausoleum, the ancient theatre has been completely restored. It was started by Mausolus, extensively adapted by the Romans, and is now used to stage events during the town's autumn festival. The view is somewhat marred by the noise from the main road.

Bodrum's restored ancient theatre

Round trip from Bodrum

Catch the morning car ferry from Bodrum to Körmen. The tourist office has ferry departure times. From here it is a 10-minute drive across the peninsula to the town of Datça (► 65).

On the way to Datça, a signposted road on the right leads west to Knidos (► 76) at the end of the peninsula. The road is not a good one, however, so unless you cannot wait to get there by boat, carry straight on here to Datça.

Distance
185km (115 miles)

Time
3–5 hours; full day if you decide to visit Knidos to swim

Start/end point
Bodrum
30B2

Lunch
Plenty of choice in town (£–££)

Turn left to take the main road (400) to Marmaris (about one hour's drive).

Marmaris (► 80–1) is the best place to stop for lunch.

From Marmaris, follow the signs inland to Muğla.

Beehives are dotted about in the surrounding forest: this is where the renowned pine-scented honey of Marmaris comes from.

Collecting the famous Marmaris honey

About 15km (9 miles) after passing a right turn to Fethiye, turn off the main road, following the signpost to Muğla.

Alexander the Great marched his army through this mountain pass, but your vehicle will make the journey in far less time. There are fine views of the Gulf of Gökova, with space to park and take in the scenery.

From Muğla (► 83), follow signs to Yatağan, which will bring you back to the main Bodrum road. At Yatağan follow signs for Milas (► 83) and from there turn south for Bodrum.

Below: *The beach at Calış is a quiet alternative to the ever-busy Ölüdeniz*

What to see in the Southern Aegean

- 30B2
- 5km south of Didyma
- Tourist restaurants (£–££)
- *Dolmuş*/minibus from Kuşadası
- Didyma (➤ 66)

ALTINKUM

'Lazy by day, lively by night' is one travel brochure's catch-phrase for this popular package-holiday destination. The 1km (half a mile) beach is popular, especially with British visitors, the whole area is a building site as developers fling up huge Costa del Sol type estates—some 25,000 Brits have moved in so far. There are tourist restaurants and a modern shopping centre specialising in goods such as watches and designer-label clothes. Of more enduring value, the superb temple of Apollo at Didyma (➤ 66) is just five minutes' drive up the road.

- 30B1
- 30km west of Marmaris
- Quayside restaurants (£–££)
- *Dolmuş*/minibus from Marmaris

BOZBURUN

This is not a typical Turkish Aegean seaside village. There is a harbour but no beach. It has a range of accommodation, and a number of good restaurants patronized by well-off city families. Boats stop here for lunch, and there is good swimming from the rocks.

- 30C1
- 5km north of Fethiye
- Restaurants (£–££)
- *Dolmuş*/minibus or ferry *dolmuş* from Fethiye
- Fethiye (➤ 68–69), Hisarönü (➤ 73)

CALIŞ

This is the nearest beach, albeit a shingle one, to Fethiye, and the two places are linked by regular public transport on road and sea. The beach stretches for 2km (1 mile), and runs parallel to the road, which is closed to traffic in the high season. There is the usual array of hotels, bars and restaurants but on the whole Calış is a lot quieter and more pleasant than nearby Hisarönü.

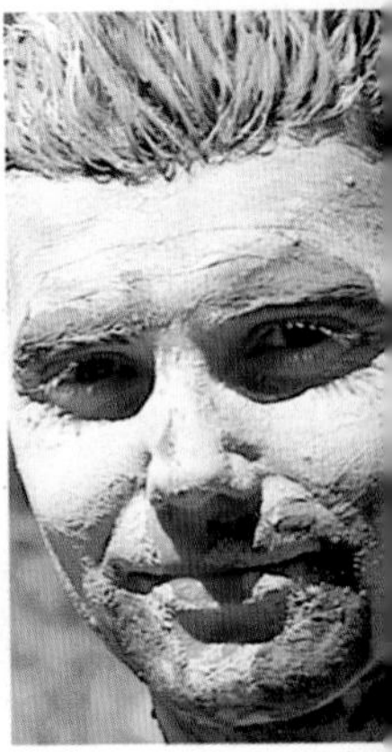

Above and left: *Enjoy slapping on some healthy mud at Dalyan*

DALYAN

✪✪

Dalyan is close to an airport and the main coast road, with Marmaris to the west and the sites of ancient Lycia to the east. Boats leave the quayside every morning before 10 to make the 40-minute journey to İstuzu beach, which is excellent for swimming as well as being a nesting site of the loggerhead turtle between May and October. Development has been prohibited here because the young turtles seem to be confused by bright lights. You can spend a day at İstuzu and return at half-hourly intervals in the afternoon. The beach has little shade, so take hats and suncream. Another popular excursion is a ten-minute boat ride upriver to thermal baths at Ilıca. A wallow in the open-air mud pools, which reach a temperature of 40°C/104°F, is said to do the body a power of good. In cooler months it is pleasant to hire a bicycle in Dalyan and cycle to the ancient ruins at Kaunos (➤ 75).

- 30C2
- 13km (8 miles) south of the main Muğla–Fethiye road
- Restaurants (£–££)
- *Dolmuş*/minibus to Marmaris, Muğla and Fethiye
- Kaunos (➤ 75), Köyceğiz (➤ 76)
- Day tours from Dalyan combine İstuzu beach, Kaunos and Köyceğiz

DATÇA

✪

This town, centrally located along the long and narrow peninsula that stretches west from Marmaris, has most of its shops and facilities laid out along one long main street. The harbour is attracting a growing number of yachts, and the town is slowly developing services for tourists: hotels, restaurants and bars with music are dotted along the seafront. Boat trips go to ancient Knidos and to various swimming places away from the town itself. The best place for swimming close to town is at the far side of the west beach.

- 30B2
- 75km 46.5 miles) west of Marmaris
- In centre ☎ (0252) 712 3163
- Restaurants (£–££)
- *Dolmuş*/minibus from Marmaris and Muğla, car ferry from Körmen, 9km north, to Bodrum (➤ 63)
- Knidos (➤ 76), Marmaris (➤ 80–81)

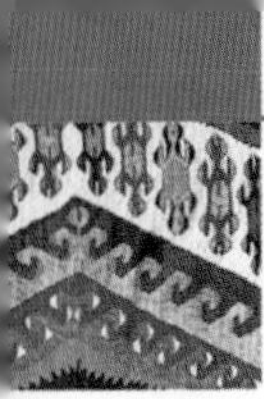

Medusa, despite the serpents in her hair, was loved by Poseidon

DİDİM (DIDYMA)

This stupendous temple of Apollo, built to house an oracle, should not be missed. The Persians destroyed one temple here in the late fifth century BC, and the one that now looms dramatically by the side of the road was begun about 300BC. A British archaeologist in the 19th century described the remains as 'piled up like shattered icebergs', but excellent restoration work has revealed the temple's mighty proportions and splendour. Be sure to walk to the back of the structure where one of the fallen columns has been preserved by archaeologists to show how it tumbled apart after falling. At the site entrance is an imposing head of Medusa, once part of a richly decorated frieze.

Steps lead up to the main platform and its 12 columns, and from here two tunnels lead down to the cellar. At the far side stood a small building where the cult statue resided. Here, next to the oracular spring, the prophetess delivered her utterances to the temple priests, who wrote them down and presented them to the client. Some fragments of the inscribed prophecies have been found, but it is likely that most were destroyed by Christians who built a church inside the temple itself. The Romans built a stadium so close to the south that the bottom steps on this side of the temple were used as seats. Many names, carved on the seats to reserve places, can still be clearly made out. After visiting the temple, have a drink on the veranda of the Oracle *pansiyon* directly overlooking the west side of the site.

- 30B2
- 75km (46.5 miles) south of Kuşadası
- 0256 813 1968
- Daily 8.30–5.30
- Two restaurants (£) opposite site entrance
- *Dolmuş*/minibus from Söke
- None
- Inexpensive
- Altınkum (➤ 64), Miletos (➤ 50), Priene (➤ 52)
- Tours from Kuşadası combine Miletos, Priene and Didyma

Fethiye

This walk starts at the tourist office (► 68) where you can collect a town map. After leaving the tourist office, turn right.

After 100m (110 yards) you will pass the town's Roman theatre on the right (► 68). At the roundabout just ahead, take the inland street, by following the blue sign for Sokak 45.

You will soon pass a Turkish bath (► 115) and the Car Cemetery pub, opposite each other, while the Music Factory is a few doors down. At the end of the street have a look in the Ottoman Café (► 113).

Then turn left. Go down to the T-junction with the Atatürk statue and turn to the right, crossing to the other side of the street.

Distance
5km (3 miles)

Time
2–3 hours

Start point
Tourist office
30C1

End point
Sesa Park Hotel
30C1

Lunch
Sesa Park Hotel
Akdeniz Caddesi 17
0252 614 4656

Just before the PTT (post office), a Lycian sarcophagus can be seen on the left (► 68).

Stay on the main road until you reach a gleaming mosque and at this junction turn right and walk up the cobbled street. At the T-junction, go left and cross to the other side. After a few hundred metres, turn right at a yellow sign for Kayaköy. Turn right at the top, and then left at the playground to walk up through houses to the site entrance for the Lycian rock tombs (► 25). To continue the walk, retrace your steps to the junction by the mosque and carry straight across and down Hastane Caddesi, towards the sea, and have lunch in the hotel at the end of the street.

Cut into the rocky hillface overlooking Fethiye, some of the tombs can be reached on foot from the streets below

30B2
Between Lake Bafa and Milas, 2km (1 mile) southeast of Selimiye
24 hours
Dolmuş/minibus from Milas
None
Inexpensive
Milas (➤ 83), Iasos (➤ 73), Herakleıa (➤ 45)

EUROMOS ✪✪

The only substantial remnant of the ancient city of Euromos is its Temple of Zeus, but its setting among olive groves is so picturesque and the remains so evocative that it is well worth making the short detour if you are travelling between Milas and Kuşadası. Euromos was founded in the sixth century BC, and the temple owes its existence to the patronage of the Romans, probably Emperor Hadrian (AD117–38). The city itself was built half a kilometre to the northwest of the temple but there is little to see.

30C1
170km east of Marmaris, 80km (50 miles) northwest of Kalkan
Near harbour, İskele Meydan 1 ☎ 0252 614 1527

Museum
Tue–Sun 8.30–12, 1–5.30
Restaurants (£–££)
Bus to Denizli, İzmir, Kalkan, Marmaris, Pamukkale, Patara, Xanthos
Kayaköy (➤ 75) Ölüdeniz (➤ 21), Calış (➤ 64), Hisarönü (➤ 73), Xanthos (➤ 26), Letoön (➤ 77), Pınara (➤ 85), Tlos (➤ 88)

FETHİYE ✪✪

The modern town of Fethiye, occupying the site of ancient Telmessos, was completely rebuilt after a devastating earthquake in 1957, and the modern quayside and promenade stand on the rubble of the old city. There had been an earlier earthquake in 1857, so very little is left of ancient Telmessos.

Nothing is known about its origins, but it became part of Lycia, fell to Alexander in due course and was later ruled by Rome. Apart from the Lycian rock tombs (➤ 25) and an excavated Roman theatre near the tourist office (both easily taken in on an early morning walk through town, ➤ 67), the best reminder of ancient Telmessos is next to the post office in the centre of town. Here sits a large, double-fronted sarcophagus with an arched lid, carrying fading reliefs of Lycian warriors. At the end of the 19th century it stood in the sea, but the fall of the sea level has returned it to dry land.

Although Fethiye is clearly a resort town, it is quite different from Bodrum or Marmaris. Less sophisticated, it has managed to avoid intense commercialism, retaining a recognisably Turkish character.

Like Bodrum and Marmaris, however, it has a quayside that bustles with activity each morning as tourists take their seats for one of the popular boat excursions to nearby beaches and islands. It also has plenty of restaurants and hotels for visitors, lively bars, a Turkish bath (► 115), and lovely golden sandy beaches in the vicinity. Fethiye also makes a good base for visiting a number of major and minor ancient sites, or for an excursion to the ghost town of Kayaköy (► 75).

There is a small **museum** in the centre of town with some interesting archaeological finds from Letoön and Patara. The main bus station is 2km (1 mile) to the east of the town, and a *dolmuş* station, in the centre of town behind the mosque, serves the local beaches. The bus company, 'Pamukkale', also has offices in the centre of town, so it is relatively straightforward to book long-distance bus journeys.

Ölüdeniz (► 21) is, justifiably, the most popular and famous of the local beaches, but there are others near by at Calış and Hisarönü. There are 12 islands dotting Fethiye Bay, and boat trips visit some of these for swimming and exploring.

Left: *The idyllic location adds charm to the Temple of Zeus at Euromos*

Boat trips depart from Fethiye every morning to beaches and islands

In the Know

If you only have a short time to visit western Turkey, or would like to get a real flavour of the region, here are some ideas:

10 Ways to Be a Local

Drink tea without milk throughout the day from tiny, tulip-shaped glasses.
Express a negative by slightly raising your head and eyes upwards and tutt-tutting.
Remove shoes before entering a mosque, and be modestly dressed. Women should cover their hair.
Relieve stress by using a set of worry beads.
Splash the proffered cologne around neck and face on long-distance buses.
Men should have a shave in a traditional hairdressing salon.
Play backgammon on the street and be prepared for a return game.

Tolerate smoking, even in no-smoking areas. Turkey is a land of smokers.
Drink bottled mineral water rather than tap water, which tastes unpleasant.
Observe the Mediterranean custom of *piyasa vakti* ('plaza time') by dressing smartly, strolling through town and along the seafront in the evening, and indulging in aimless conversation.

10 Good Places to Have Lunch

Agora (£) ✉ Herakleıa ☎ 0252 543 5445 The smartest of the small number of restaurants in Herakleia, serving Turkish and some Western dishes in a pleasant outdoor setting under shade.
La Dolce Vita (££) ✉ Hilton Hotel, Gaziosmanpasa Bulvarı, İzmir ☎ 0232 441 6060 Air-conditioned comfort in which to sample pizzas and Caesar salad from an international menu. Some tables are placed near the street for outdoor dining.
Efes Pub (£) ✉ SSK İşhanı 07, Konak, İzmir ☎ 0232 484 7036 ⏲ 8AM–midnight. Conveniently close to the museums and bazaar, this licensed restaurant and bar is a good place for lamb chops and steaks and a range of light salad-based meals.
İelgle (£) ✉ Güllübahçe ☎ 0256 547 1009 The small waterfall alongside this restaurant adds to its charm. The menu offers fish dishes, kebabs, steak or meatballs. An ideal stopping point before or after a visit to ancient Priene.
Kalehan (£) ✉ Kalehan Hotel, Atatürk Caddesi 49, Selçuk ☎ 0232 892 6154 The only restaurant in Selçuk with some character to its surroundings, plus the comfort of air-conditioning and good Turkish food. The à la carte menu changes daily, the four-course set meals are good value, and there is a wine list.
Körfez (£) ✉ Seafront, Çeşme ☎ 0232)712 6718 This sea-facing restaurant has a large menu but it is the fish or fish-based dishes which are the most tempting. There is an impressive selection of *meze*, as well as the main fish dishes. There are also 'International cuisine selections' for those who prefer chicken curry or steak and chips.
Labranda ✉ 21km (13 miles) off the Milas-Selçuk road. Take a picnic with you up to the remote ruins at Labranda (➤ 77). The road is not easy but the rewards are truly spectacular with cool shaded woodland fringing vast panoramas.

Sardis (Sart) (£) ✉ Near Salihli 9km (5.5 miles) from Sardis. Have lunch with the Turkish truck drivers at one of the *köfte* restaurants near Salihli. You eat what you are given sausage, *köftesı* (meatballs) and bread, no one speaks English, but the welcome is friendly.
Rihtim (£) ✉ Çanakkale ☎ 0286 217 1770 There are other restaurants alongside the Rihtim, but this is one of the longer-established places on the quayside street facing the Dardanelles. The speciality is fish, served with salad and chips, but other dishes are on the menu.
Villa Pizza (£) ✉ Çarşi Caddesi Fethiye ☎ 0252 614 6451 There's a choice here of two dozen pizzas, half meat and half vegetarian. It's just round the corner from the Ottoman Café. For Turkish cuisine try Meğri at No 13 on the same street.

10 Top Activities

Boating: hire a boat, join a cruise or charter a boat with a crew.
Go underwater: use a snorkel or dive – resorts have facilities for all levels of experience.
Swim: huge choice of beaches (▶ 110).
Visit ancient sites: Ephesus (▶ 41–3) and other popular sites have the most to see, but less famous ones may have more atmosphere.
Visit a Greek island: for example Rhodes from Marmaris (▶ 82).
Walk: the best way to see the wildlife and landscape.
Shop: all day and half the night. Shops stay open late (▶ 104–9).
Watch the wildlife: loggerhead turtles on beaches, storks on buildings, lizards and tortoises at ancient sites, wild flowers everywhere.
Enjoy the nightlife: summer is a non-stop party at the big resorts.
Watch the ancient art of camel-wrestling: usually between late October and March, especially popular in the Selçuk area.

10 Best Buys

- **Carpets** are sold everywhere.
- **Ceramic** plates, bowls, jugs and pots come in vivid blues and greens with abstract designs.
- A **brass tea tray**, complete with tiny tea glasses.
- **Designer-label clothes**.
- **Food**: pine-scented honey, bags of pine nuts, gift-wrapped pastries and Turkish delight.
- **Leather** jackets, coats, shoes, bags and belts.
- **Meerschaum** is a soft white magnesium silicate from western Anatolia, carved by craftsmen into pipes and figurines.
- **Onyx** is best purchased from a workshop where you see the quartz being cut and shaped. Inexpensive, but very heavy.
- An **Ottoman-style** souvenir, perhaps a water pipe, copperware or jewellery.
- ***Raki***: a bottle or two.

Relieve stress with a set of worry beads

Boat trips in a traditional gület *are available from most coastal resorts*

- 30B2
- Between Bodrum and Marmaris
- Boats and yachts from Bodrum and Marmaris
- Moderate–expensive, depending on the length of cruise
- Bodrum (➤ 58–62), Marmaris (➤ 80–81)

GÖKOVA KÖRFEZI (GULF OF GÖKOVA)

Bodrum is the most popular departure point for a 'turquoise cruise' or 'blue voyage' along the beautiful, 56km coastline of the Gulf of Gökova. *Gülets*, the traditional broad-beamed vessels of the area, can be chartered with a crew, and watersports equipment is usually included. Destinations include Yedi Adalar, a quiet bay on the southeast corner of the gulf and Sideyri Adası (Cedar Island, ➤ 85), with the beach that Anthony is supposed to have created for Cleopatra.

- 30B2
- 2km (1 mile) west of Bodrum
- Restaurants (£–££)
- *Dolmuş*/minibus from Bodrum
- Bodrum (➤ 58–62), Gümüşlük (➤ 73), Turgutreis (➤ 89)

GÜMBET

This beach, the closest one to Bodrum, has become a self-contained resort, and is very popular with young people on two-week package holidays. There are hotels, pubs, nightclubs and restaurants in abundance; the 600-m (656-yd) long beach is not superb but even so you cannot be sure of finding a space in high summer. The best thing about Gümbet is the range of water-based sports and activities available on the beach.

GÜMÜŞLÜK

A photogenic fishing village, half an hour's drive from Bodrum, Gümüşlük has, like the rest of the peninsula, been overrun by tourism. The village is on the site of ancient Myndos and this has resulted in restrictions being imposed on new buildings. The fish restaurants (➤ 98) along the waterfront are not inexpensive but they make a delightful stop. The 1-km (half a mile) long beach is a mixture of sand and gravel, and swimming in the sea at the south end brings you close to some Myndos ruins.

- 30B2
- 15km (9 miles) west of Bodrum
- Fish restaurants (££–£££)
- *Dolmuş*/minibus from Bodrum
- Bodrum (➤ 58–62), Turgutreis (➤ 89), Yalıkavak (➤ 90), Gümbet (➤ 72), Ortakent (➤ 84)

HISARÖNÜ AND OVACIK

Hisarönü and Ovacık are close to the coast, though not actually on it, and are busily developing as accommodation centres for the Fethiye region. Hisarönü, the larger and more popular of the two resorts, is very much a tourist satellite settlement for Ölüdeniz, 4km (2.5 miles) away down the hillside. Fish and chip shops testify to Hisarönü's popularity with the British; for a quieter destination, nearby Calış (➤ 64) is preferable. New bars and restaurants are opening in both Hisarönü and Ovacık, with a better choice of fare than the eating places on the beaches.

- 30C1
- 10km (6 miles) south of Fethiye
- Bars and restaurants (£–££)
- *Dolmuş*/minibus from Fethiye
- Kayaköy (➤ 75) Ölüdeniz (➤ 21), Calış (➤ 64), Lycian Rock Tombs (➤ 25), Xanthos (➤ 26), Letoön (➤ 77), Pınara (➤ 85), Tlos (➤ 88)

İASOS

Populated from around 2000BC, ancient İasos prospered under the Romans, and in Byzantine times the Knights of St. John built a castle here. The last vestiges of the town lie by the side of the village of Kıyıkışlacık, whose name translates as 'the little barracks on the coast'. Most of what can still be seen belongs to the second century AD, including the remains of a Roman mausoleum and a *bouleuterion* (meeting hall), but it takes something of a leap of the imagination to picture them in their complete state. The Byzantine castle is the most impressive sight and gives fine views. A small museum stands over the mausoleum, and its fragmented exhibits found on the site are poignant reminders of the almost-vanished town.

- 30B2
- Kıyıkışlacık, 8km (5 miles) north west of Milas, 4km (2.5 miles) southeast of Euromos
- Tue–Sun 8–12, 1–5.30
- Fish restaurants (£) in Kıyıkışlacık
- *Dolmuş*/minibus from Milas or boat from Güllük
- Inexpensive
- Milas (➤ 83), Euromos (➤ 68)

Left: *Diners can get their feet wet at the fish restaurants in Gümüşlük*

- 30B2
- 8km (5 miles) south of Marmaris
- Tourist restaurants (£–££)
- *Dolmuş*/minibus, or ferry *dolmuş*, from Marmaris
- Marmaris (➤ 80–81), Turunç (➤ 89), Bozburun (➤ 64), Datça (➤ 65), Ródos (Rhodes, ➤ 82)

İçmeler is a quieter place than its near neighbour Marmaris

İÇMELER

The gap between Marmaris and the resort of İçmeler is getting smaller all the time, but there is still a qualitative difference between the two towns.

İçmeler has a more sedate character: the nightclubs tend to close earlier, there is little in the way of budget accommodation, and the typical summer visitor is more likely to be older. An 8-km (5-mile) beach links the two resorts. Despite it being municipal property and open to all, most of the hotels backing on to the beach try to claim a patch by filling it with their deckchairs.

You can make the half-hour journey by *dolmuş* ferry, the last stop from Marmaris being at the back of the Munumar Vista Hotel (➤ 103).

KALKAN ✪✪

Coming from Fethiye, the road suddenly reaches the top of a cliff and looks down to a little town hugging the cliffs in the curve of a bay. A well-kept secret among seasoned budget travellers until tourism made its impact in the early 1980s, Kalkan is growing rapidly, but is still a pleasant, and more sophisticated, alternative to Fethiye as a base for exploring this corner of the coast. The town's picturesque houses seem precariously attached to the hillside and there are steep cobbled streets, a pebble-beached cove, a good range of accommodation and decent restaurants.

30C1
80km east of Fethiye
Restaurants (£–££)
Dolmuş/minibus from Fethiye and Kas
None: steep streets are unavoidable
Xanthos (► 26), Letoön (► 77), Pınara (► 85), Tlos (► 88)

KAUNOS ✪

Ancient Kaunos was founded in the ninth century BC, and its ruins make an worthwhile excursion by boat from nearby Dalyan. Originally a Carian city, Kaunos came under the cultural influence of neighbouring Lycia, and this is apparent in its decorated rock tombs, which resemble the Lycian tombs at Fethiye (► 25). Archaeological work is still going on at Kaunos; the ruins include well-preserved sections of wall from the fourth century BC, and a theatre which was built some 200 years later. In ancient times the Mediterranean came right up to the acropolis, but the marshland that now attracts mosquitoes (bring repellent) must have been in evidence in the past: Herodotus noted that the inhabitants were reputed to have yellowish skin, probably caused by malaria.

30C2
Dalyan (► 65)
Daily 8.30–5.30
Dolmuş/minibus from Marmaris, Muğla and Fethiye or boat from Dalyan
Inexpensive
Dalyan (► 65), Köyceğiz (► 76)
Day tours from Dalyan

The rock tombs of Kaunos are best seen on one of the regular boat trips

KAYAKÖY ✪✪

This town of some 2,000 homes, once called *Levissi*, lost its Greek Orthodox inhabitants in 1923 in the exchange of populations that followed the War of Independence (► 11). Now a UNESCO World Heritage Site, it is being restored as an historic village. So far it has a few *pensiyons* and wine bars. Louis de Bernière based his book, *Birds Without Wings*, on it.

30C1
7km (4 miles) south of Fethiye
Restaurants and cafés (£)
Dolmuş/minibus from Fethiye
Fethiye (► 68–69), Ölüdeniz (► 21)

30B1
35km (22 miles) west of Datça
Daily 8–7
Fish restaurants (£–££) near dock
Boat from Datça or Mamaris
None Inexpensive
Datça (➤ 65)

Below: *ruined Knidos has a dramatic location*

KNİDOS

The location is an appealing one—the exposed tip of the spiny Marmaris peninsula—and the ancient city of Cnidus was built here to benefit the Mediterranean sea trade. The settlement grew rich and famous, and at one time its proudest inhabitant was a statue of Aphrodite, carved by Praxiteles, the Michelangelo of the time. The statue has disappeared but there are various remnants of the old city, spread over a wide area: the most substantial are the Hellenistic theatre and the Byzantine basilicas, and you can also see the remains of a lighthouse and necropolis. The view is spellbinding, with a number of Greek islands, Ródos (Rhodes), Cos, Yiali, Nisiros and Khalki visible from the ruins. A rough road leads to Knidos (➤ 63), but it is much more pleasant to take a boat from Datça. Day-long boat trips include stops for lunch and a swim.

Did you know ?

The statue of Aphrodite that once adorned Knidos was a major tourist attraction in its time. It was considered to be one of the world's finest works of art and may have been the first free-standing sculpture of a female nude in Greece. It is thought to have been destroyed by Christians in the Byzantine era; copies survive in European cities and New York.

30C2
50km (31 miles) east of the Muğla–Marmaris road
Restaurants (£–££)
Dolmuş/minibus from Marmaris and Muğla
Main square 0252 262 4703 Mon–Fri 8.30–12.30
Dalyan (➤ 65), Kaunos (➤ 75)

KÖYCEĞIZ

A peaceful inland town on Lake Köyceğiz, without the intense commercialism of coastal resorts, Köyceğiz has a modest appeal. The lake is the centre of attraction and there are regular boat excursions to the opposite shore, where you can bathe in the life-enhancing mud of the Sultaniye Kaplıcaları. These thermal baths, rich in calcium, potassium and sulphur, attract far fewer visitors than those at Ilıca and also benefit from a more interesting setting. Boats also cross the lake to Daylan and Kaunos: ask at the tourist office in the main square for details.

LABRANDA ✪✪

The sanctuary of Zeus at Labranda is not easy to reach, even with your own car, but the effort is richly rewarded. A few miles outside Milas, on the main road heading north to Selçuk, the turn-off is signposted on the right. The site is 14km (9 miles) further on, and the paved road ends after 6km (4 miles) at the village of Karigeak. It is not advisable to try the drive in winter unless it is very dry. Swedish archaeologists has done some work here at Labranda, and the main ruins are clearly marked. The most interesting are the two structures where devotees held their sacrificial banquets, and an impressive fourth century BC tomb. The isolated setting and the sweeping views afforded by the steep location of these little-visited ruins make this one of the more evocative ancient sites of the Turkish Aegean.

- 30B2
- 17km (10.5 miles) north of Milas
- Daily 8–8
- Car or taxi from Milas
- None
- Inexpensive
- Euromos (➤ 68), Iasos (➤ 73), Milas (➤ 83)

LETOÖN ✪

Letoön, the Lycian centre for the worship of Leto, was an important sanctuary in ancient times. First excavated in 1962, the remains of three third century BC temples, dedicated to Leto, Artemis and Apollo, bear testimony to its significance. Leto was a nymph who was loved by Zeus, and was jealously hounded by his wife Hera as a consequence. Wolves guided the preganant Leto to the River Xanthos, where she bathed and renamed the place Lycia (from the Greek for wolf, *lykos*) before giving birth to Artemis and Apollo. Alexander the Great came here and received encouragement for his imminent battle against the Persians. There is also a Hellenistic theatre and an inscription found here was instrumental in the eventual deciphering of the Lycian language.

- 30C1
- Kumluova, 6km southwest of Xanthos
- Daily 8.30–5
- *Dolmuş*/minibus from Fethiye to Kumluova
- None
- Inexpensive
- Xanthos (➤ 26, 90), Kalkan (➤ 75), Pınara (➤ 85), Tlos (➤ 88)

Letoön was the most important religious centre in ancient Lycia

Marmaris to Pamukkale

Leave Marmaris, following signs for Muğla.

About 12km (7.5 miles) after passing the right turn for Fethiye, the road climbs through a mountain pass to reach Muğla (➤ 83), and there are splendid views of the Gulf of Gökova (➤ 72).

As you approach the ring road at Muğla, follow signs to Denizli.

The road (330) to Denizli is over 100km (62 miles) along a scenic route which is very much off the beaten tourist track. The changing colours of the landscape as the road weaves its way towards the village of Kale are enchanting.

Distance
150km/93 miles (excluding Aphrodisias)

Time
4–5 hours

Start point
Marmaris
30B2

End point
Pamukkale
30C3

Lunch
Anatolia Restaurant, Afrodisias (➤ 16)

From Kale the road continues to Tavas. Turn left if you want to make a diversion (60km/37 miles return) to Afrodisias (➤ 34). If not, follow the Afyon/Ankara road out of Denizli and after about 8km (5 miles) take the left turn, signposted to Pamukkale.

Very soon after this turning, just before the village of Korucuk, there is a left turn signposted to Laodikeiá (➤ 49). Save this visit for later and press on to Pamukkale (➤ 22–3). This is the best place for lunch, after which you can explore Hierapolis (➤ 20).

In the evening, if time allows, it does not take long to drive down to Laodikeiá. If you turn left onto the main road in the direction of Ankara, it is less than 2km (1 mile) to a crumbling old caravanserai on the left side of the road as you reach the bottom of a hill.

Left: *social time on the beach and* (above) *time to yourself at a classical site*

Mooring space is at a premium in Marmaris harbour

MARMARİS ✪✪

Set by the side of an 8-km (5-mile) long bay and framed by pine forests and oleander shrubs, Marmaris looks out to sea where the Aegean and the Mediterranean meet. The town's name is said to come from a remark by Süleyman the Magnificent in 1522—*mimari* translates as 'hang the architect'. He was unimpressed by the fortress he was using for an attack on the Knights of St. John at Rhodes. In 1798, the British Admiral Nelson used the bay to prepare his fleet for an attack on the French at Abukir.

Along with Kuşadası and Bodrum, Marmaris is one of the big three coastal resorts on the Turkish Aegean, and manages to satisfy most modern visitors. There is a strong contingent of young people who are here to party, and as in Kuşadası, one of the roads has become known as Bar Street. Families come here on package holidays, which often include free accommodation for children, and many of the hotels have a children's pool and play area. Marmaris also has a very large and modern marina with a highly affluent clientele, hence the expensive restaurants around town. Other visitors find that neighbouring İçmeler, now virtually a suburb, is ideal as a quieter accommodation base, while still being handy for shopping in Marmaris' excellent bazaar and sightseeing in the area.

Choose a carpet carefully and take the sales talk with a pinch of salt

The town may lack Bodrum's air of sophistication, but a stroll along the promenade at dusk does have its charms. Islands and coves can be made out in the bay, scores of brightly painted boats nod at their moorings, and chains of twinkling lights enhance the scene. Restaurants, bars and cafés line the pedestrianized road and tempt you to take a seat under the palm trees.

The statue of Atatürk near the waterfront is the hub of the town centre. The statue divides the two main streets that face the harbour, Atatürk Caddesi to the west and Kordon Caddesi to the east.The main inland road that comes down to meet the statue is Ulusal Egemenlik Bulvarı. Most places of interest are to the east of the statue, and Kordon Caddesi leads to the tourist office, banks, post office and shops.

There is a small **museum** behind the tourist office, but most visitors prefer to check out the shops or organize day trips to the nearby islands of Rhodes, Kaunos or Knidos and numerous other destinations, either by sea or land.

30B2

170km (105 miles) west of Fethiye, 165km (102 miles) east of Bodrum

Restaurants (£–£££)

Buses from Bodrum, Fethiye, İzmir, Pamukkale

Iskele Meydanı 0252 313 0722 Daily 8–7.30, summer; Mon–Fri 8–12, 1–5, winter

İçmeler (➤ 74), Turunç (➤ 89), Bozburun (➤ 64), Datça (➤ 65), Rhodes (➤ 82)

Museum

Daily 8–12, 1–5

Inexpensive

Distinctive blue and white beehives produce some of Turkey's best honey

Did you know ?

The lines of blue and white beehives in the Marmaris area, usually lying flat on the ground, produce some of the best honey in Turkey. Be sure to sample the dark-coloured çam balı *variety, distinguished by its pine scent that comes from the forests where the hives are placed.*

Ródos (Rhodes)

Distance
Approximately 80km (50 miles) return trip

Time
Crossing takes 45 minutes. Allow all day to explore town

Start/end point
Marmaris harbour
30B2

Lunch
Plenty of choice (£–££)

City of Rhodes Tourist Office 022410 23655/23255 Daily 8.30am–9pm

With a day return ticket there are no taxes to pay and you don't need a visa. Take your passport, though, and don't forget to check the times of the last boat back. Note you will need to pay for another Turkish visa on re-entering Turkey, in cash, hard currency only.

Take the hydrofoil from Marmaris harbour. You can buy tickets in advance from one of the travel agencies on Kordon Caddesi.

The 45-minute journey will take you to the Mandraki harbour in the more modern part of Rhodes Town, the capital of this popular Greek island. The Colossus of Rhodes, one of the Seven Wonders of the Ancient World, is believed to have stood over the entrance to this harbour.

After disembarking, make your way to the tourist office in the Plateía Riminí, north of the medieval town.

From here you can explore the old town, mainly a product of occupation by the Knights Hospitallers of St. John. They occupied the island from 1306 (after losing control of Jerusalem) to 1522, when they capitulated to Süleyman the Magnificent's Turkish army after a seige lasting for 177 days. As well as touring the medieval walls, the Palace of the Grand Masters and the Byzantine and Archaeological museums are well worth visiting. There are plenty of fascinating mosques, old streets and shopping opportunities to keep you occupied all day.

When you have had enough of the bustle, return to Mandraki harbour for the hydrofoil back to Marmaris.

There are many quiet alleys in the medieval quarter of Rhodes Town

MİLAS ✪

This agricultural town and centre of carpet production was the site of ancient Mylasa and capital of the Carian kingdom. Follow the main street, Kadıağa Caddesi, which becomes Gümüşkesen Caddesi, to reach the large Roman tomb known as the Gümüşkesen, about 1km (half a mile) west of the town centre. It may be a copy on a smaller scale of the Mausoleum of Halicarnassus (Bodrum, ➤ 61). Retrace your route to the very beginning of Kadıağa Caddesi, on the east side of town near the canal, where there is an attractive 14th-century mosque, the Ulu Cami. Take the road north from here for about 250m (273yds), and the Baltalı Kapı will come into view. Known as the Gate with an Axe, this Roman gate has a double-headed axe carved into a stone on the north side.

- 30B2
- 45km (30 miles) northeast of Bodrum
- Restaurants (£)
- Buses from Marmaris and Kuşadası
- Euromos (➤ 68), Iasos (➤ 73), Labranda (➤ 77)
- Milas–Bodrum Airport ☎ 0252 523 0101

MUĞLA ✪

Start by calling at the tourist office and collecting a town map; this is a town to walk around at a leisurely pace, taking in the general air of prosperity.

The most interesting area to explore is the old Ottoman quarter, with its winding streets of pretty buildings. From the tourist office by the Atatürk statue, head north up Kurşunlu Caddesi and take a look in at Yağcıar Hanı, a modern shopping centre in a converted caravanserai. The street continues north up to the town's bazaar, also worth visiting, and higher up on the hillside are many photogenic houses. These are well-preserved examples of domestic Ottoman architecture.

- 30C2
- 73km (45 miles) north of Marmaris
- Restaurants (£) in the centre of town
- *Dolmuş*/minibus to Bodrum, Denizli, İzmir, Marmaris
- Emirbeyazıt Mah ☎ 0252 214 1261; www.mugla-turizm.gov.tr Mon–Fri 8–7, summer; Mon–Fri 8–12, 1–5, winter

ÖLÜDENIZ (➤ 21, TOP TEN)

One of the many attractive examples of Ottoman architecture in Muğla

ÖREN

30B2
55km (34 miles) south of Milas
Restaurants (£) near beach
Occasional *dolmuş*/minibus from Milas

Byzantine fortress
Daily 8am–dusk
Inexpensive

It is easy to miss Ören: after leaving Milas and travelling south for 3km (2 miles), look for the main junction where the road goes right for Bodrum. Turn left instead for Muğla; the turn for Ören is very soon after on the right. Ören is a pleasant coastal village, used more by Turkish families than foreign holidaymakers, with an attractive 1km pebbly beach, and the scant remains of the ancient city of Ceramus. Public transport is infrequent, and it is best to drive yourself. The **Byzantine fortress** here is a good place for a picnic, although you will have to pay to get in.

ORTAKENT

30B2
10km (6 miles) west of Bodrum
Restaurants (£–££)
Dolmuş/minibus to Bodrum
Bodrum (➤ 58–62), Gümüşlük (➤ 73), Turgutreis (➤ 89)

One of the better beaches on the Bodrum peninsula, Ortakent's sand stretches for 2km (1 mile). The road is closed to traffic, so it is a safe place for children. There is nothing to see or do here but enjoy the sun, sand and sea. Various watersports are available, but windsurfing is as fast as it gets here. Ortakent has become popular on a small scale with British package groups.

PATARA

30C1
7km (4 miles) south of Xanthos
Daily 7.30–7, summer; 8.30–5, winter (site)
Restaurants (£) on beach
Dolmuş/minibus to Fethiye and Kalkan
None (ancient site)
Inexpensive (ancient site)
Xanthos (➤ 26 and 90)

A very wide 18-km (11-mile) sandy beach is the great attraction of Patara; a conservation area for birds and turtles, so the beach closes at dusk. Be cautious when swimming: there are some strong currents and no shade so go prepared. The ruins of ancient Patara, an important supply base for the Romans, are 1km (half a mile) away. It was once a port, but was engulfed by sand. The highlight is undoubtedly the sand-filled theatre.

Patara has one of the best beaches in Turkey

PINARA

This is not an easy to place to reach, even with your own transport, but the journey is attractive, and lets you indulge in the illusion that you have just discovered ancient Pınara yourself. Very little is known about the place, except that it was an important Lycian city that minted its own coins. The most compelling spectacle is the openings cut into in the huge mass of rock that towers over the site. They are thought to be tombs, but access is impossible to all but dedicated rockclimbers and should not be attempted. There are other tombs at ground level and the most interesting of these, the Royal Tomb, displays fine reliefs showing people and walled settlements. Of the other ruins, the theatre is the best preserved. Bus travellers have to walk the last 5km (3 miles) from the Pınara turning.

30C1
46km (28.5 miles) southeast of Fethiye
Open 24 hours
Snacks (£) 2km (1 mile)
Dolmuş/minibus from Fethiye to Pınara turning
None
Inexpensive
Tlos (➤ 88), Sidyma (➤ 88), Xanthos (➤ 16, 90)

Above: *Ortakent, with its tall houses, nestles at the foot of a wooded hillside*

SIDEYRI ADASI (CEDAR ISLAND)

Legend has it that Mark Anthony had all the fine sand on the beach brought from northern Africa as a personal gift to the Egyptian queen: hence the name Cleopatra's Beach. The beach is the main attraction for the many people who visit on day trips from Marmaris and Bodrum. Tours from Marmaris include road transport to the boat at Çamli İskelesı. The island's name comes from the ancient city of Cedrae. It was sacked by the Spartans during the fifth-century BC Peloponnesian War, and retained its Greek culture until Arab invasions in the seventh century AD.

30B2
Gulf of Gökova
Boats from Taşbükü and Çamli İskelesı
Gulf of Gökova (➤ 72)
Tours from Marmaris include road transport to Çamli İskelesı

Food & Drink

Turkish cuisine has been open to various influences, a legacy of the far-reaching Ottoman Empire, but the underlying characteristic is a determination to conserve the natural tastes of fresh ingredients. The country imports very little food: meat, fruit and vegetables, honey and jam are all produced in Turkey.

Above: *Watermelons grow in abundance in Turkey*

Right: *A visit to a restaurant serving regional cuisine will surprise and delight*

Bread
White bread is ubiquitous—it is served with breakfast, lunch and dinner. When fresh it is soft and palatable, but it soon becomes stale. Brown bread is difficult to find in the coastal resorts, but it does exist and is worth seeking out in bakeries.

What to Eat

Breakfast usually consists of bread, honey, sheep's cheese and olives, served with tea. Depending on the class of hotel, a more substantial English or American breakfast may receive token acknowledgement in the form of cereals, cooked eggs and ham. Lunch is also a relatively light affair, with the evening meal being the main meal of the day.

Traditional starters take the form of delicious hot and cold *meze*—small dishes using a variety of ingredients, for example puréed aubergines (*patlıcan salatasi*), stuffed vine leaves (*zeytinagli yaprak dolmasi*), and finely rolled cheese

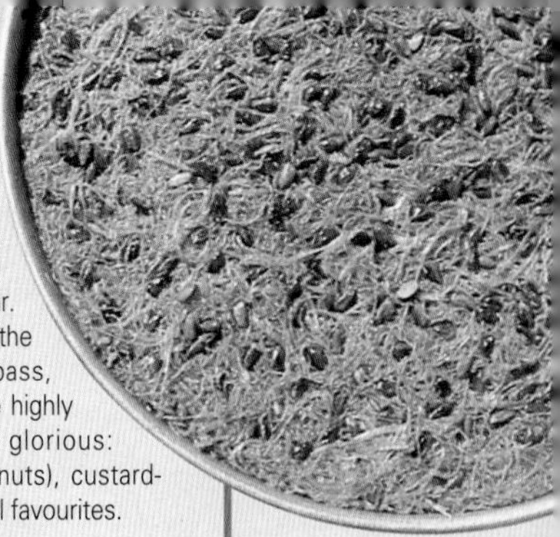

pastries (*sigara böreği*). Main dishes are usually based around lamb or beef, although boiled chicken (*tavuk*) and roast chicken (*pilav*) are also popular. Restaurants usually have fresh fish on the menus such as turbot, bream, seabass, mussels and crab. Sweet desserts are highly appreciated in Turkey, and can be glorious: *baklava* (puff pastry with syrup and nuts), custard-based desserts and rice puddings are all favourites.

Above: *Sweet, sticky desserts are very popular*

Restaurants

There are two main types of restaurant: the plain *lokanta* and the more formal *restoran*. The *lokanta* keeps its warm, previously cooked, dishes on display in steamtrays. The fare is simple but filling, usually consisting of stews, stuffed peppers, beans and rice. A *restoran* should offer a range of courses (*meze*, soup, meat dishes and desserts) and, unlike the average *lokanta*, will also serve beer and wine. There are also specialist restaurants, the names of which will indicate their speciality. The *pide salonu*, or *pideci*, offers pitta bread with various fillings, the *köftesi* serves meatballs, and the *kebapçı* concentrates on roast meat.

Something to Drink?

Tea (*çay*) is drunk throughout the day, served in tiny, gold-rimmed glasses and without milk. Apple tea (*elma çay*) is a particular favourite with the proprietors of carpet shops who wish to make potential customers feel welcome. Turkish coffee is not as common as one might expect, although Turkish people do drink it in various degrees of sweetness (*sade* is without sugar, *az* and *orta* are medium, while *çok* is saturated in sugar). The national alcohol is *raki* (➤ 98), but Turkish wine is widely available in shops and licensed restaurants. The less expensive brands will not suit everyone's palate. Locally brewed beer (*bira*) is readily available, and the Efes brand is deservedly popular with both locals and visitors. Domestically produced gin (*cin*), vodka (*vokta*) and cognac (*kanyak*) are less expensive than imported products but, other than in cocktails, the difference in taste is significant.

Turkish tea is served throughout the day and with everything

30C1
South of Eşen
None
Free
Pınara (➤ 85), Tlos (➤ 88), Letoön (➤ 77)

30C1
48km (30 miles) north of Xanthos at village of Kale Asar
24 hours
No public transport
None Inexpensive
Pınara (➤ 85), Letoön (➤ 77)

Above: *The ruins at Tlos reflect an unusually mixed heritage*

SIDYMA

This is the least visited of the Lycian sites because there is no public transport. What can be seen mostly dates back to Roman times, although there are some Lycian rock-cut tombs, a pillar tomb that has lost its grave-chamber from the top and an interesting row of sarcophagi. The site is always open.

TLOS

Ancient Tlos was one of the more important Lycian cities, and in the 19th century it became a winter headquarters for a pirate called Kanli Ali Ağa. The ruins reflect this mixed parentage. The empty remains of the pirate's fortress tower over the site from the top of the acropolis, and the Lycian remains include rock-cut tombs. If the attendant is around, ask for help in locating the best-preserved one, which has an Ionic temple façade and a relief of Bellerophon riding the winged horse, Pegasus. The theatre is also in good condition, but the baths are the most interesting of the other scattered remains.

TURGUTREİS

Turgutreis is totally dedicated to tourism, and package holiday hotels abound. There are well over 100 restaurants, and a sufficient number of bars and nightclubs to keep visitors amused for a week or longer. The parasol-peppered beach has coarse sand and, because the sea remains shallow for quite some way out, is suitable for young children.

- 30B2
- 20km (12 miles) west of Bodrum
- Restaurants (£–££)
- *Dolmuş*/minibus from Bodrum
- Bodrum (► 58–62), Gümüşlük (► 73), Yalıkavak (► 90), Gümbet (► 72)

TURUNÇ

Turunç used to be a place to escape from the crowds of Marmaris. Tourist brochures still portray the modern resort as a relaxing hideaway, but this is stretching the truth. The 500-m (545-yd) beach of coarse sand, with a splendid backdrop of cliffs and pine trees, is the focus of daily activity. It is safe for swimming and you can hire watersports equipment. Water taxis bob next to the jetties, waiting to take people to coves along the coast.

- 30B2
- 10km (6 miles) south of Marmaris
- Restaurants (£–££)
- *Dolmuş*/minibus from water *dolmuş* to Marmaris
- İçmeler (► 74), Bozburun (► 64), Datça (► 65), Marmaris (► 80–81), Rhodes (► 82)

Did you know ?

Some of the most enjoyable specialist guides to the ancient sites of western Turkey are Turkey Beyond the Meander, Lycian Turkey *and* Aegean Turkey, *written by George E Bean in the 1960s.*

Turunç is easily reached from Marmaris by minibus or water dolmuş

- 30C1
- Just north of Kınık, 63km (39 miles) from Fethiye
- Nov–end Apr daily 7.30–7; May–end Oct daily 8–5.30
- Café (£)
- *Dolmuş*/minibus from Fethiye or Kalkan
- None
- Inexpensive
- Letoön (➤ 77), Kalkan (➤ 75), Pınara (➤ 85), Tlos (➤ 88), Sidyma (➤ 88)

XANTHOS ✪✪✪

From the modern village of Kınık, on the main Fethiye–Kalkan road, it is a five-minute walk to the ancient Lycian capital of Xanthos and its Harpy Tomb (➤ 26). The acropolis overlooks the Eşen Çayi River, and it is easy to imagine the Lycians looking down on the plain in the sixth century BC as a Persian army advanced on their citadel. Rather than surrender, they set fire to their city, and those who did not die fighting perished in the flames. The ruins of the new city that arose in the fifth century BC are now the major attraction. In 42BC the Roman general, Brutus attacked the city, only to be confronted by another act of mass suicide as the Lycians realized that defeat was imminent. Under Roman rule the city thrived again, and in Byzantine times it was a centre of Christianity. A path leads to the remains of a Byzantine church, a pleasant lunch spot.

- 30B2
- 18km (11 miles) west of Bodrum
- Restaurants (£–££)
- *Dolmuş*/minibus from Marmaris
- Bodrum (➤ 58–62), Gümüşlük (➤ 73), Ortakent (➤ 84)

YALIKAVAK ✪

Tucked away on the northern shore, this is one of the less-developed of the many resorts on the Bodrum peninsula. The small town is pretty, in a manicured kind of way, with a restored 300-year-old windmill in the middle of a pedestrianized area of cobbled streets. There are far better beaches on the peninsula than Yalıkavak's pebbly one, and this helps to keep the crowds away (choose a hotel with a pool if you are staying here). Yalıkavak is ideal for people who want the facilities of bigger resorts, but not the non-stop nightlife.

Ancient amphitheatre at Xanthos

Where To...

Above: *Brooms for sale in İzmir's bazaar*
Right: *Belly dancing, like this show in Çeşme, is featured in many coastal resorts*

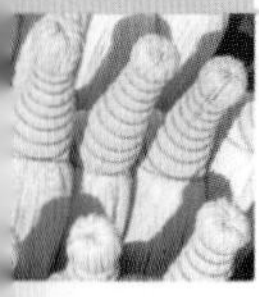

Northern Aegean

Prices

Approximate prices for a three-course meal for one person are shown by a **£** symbol:

£ = budget, under 15YTL
££ = moderate, 15–35YTL
£££ = expensive, over 35YTL

Ayvalık

Öz Canlibalik (££–£££)

There are a number of quality fish restaurants in Ayvalık, and this is one of the best. It is close to the seafront and will have whatever local fish have been recently brought in. Ask about the availability of *kidonia* and *ayvada*, two types of mussel which do not often appear on the menus of restaurants in the eastern Mediterranean. The *meze* here are also recommended.

Gazinolar Caddesi
Lunch and dinner
***Dolmuş*/minibus from Çanakkale, Assos, Bergama, İzmir**

Bergama

Sağlam (£–££)

On the main street in the centre of town, not far from the tourist office. At lunchtime there are the standard hot dishes waiting in steamtrays, but it is also worth asking about the regional dishes from Urfa. There is a small courtyard at the back for alfresco dining, and rooms upstairs.

Cumhuriyet Meydanı 29
0232 632 8897 **8–8**

Çanakkale

Aussie & Kiwi (£)

The name, the free glass of 'Milo' (a chocolate drink) with meals and the Vegemite draw in homesick Australians and New Zealanders, but anyone seeking apple crumble or a hearty breakfast will warm to this place. Fish is the best bet for a main meal. Check out the restaurant's book for comments by customers on the food, Turkey and life in general. At the Military Museum end of town.

Yali Caddesi 32 **0286 212 1722** **8am–2am May–Oct**

Trakya (£)

This restaurant has two outlets, one on each side of a square facing the main docking area where ferries cross the Dardanelles. These are *lokanta* restaurants (➤ 87) and ordering is simply a matter of pointing at whatever takes your fancy on the steamtrays. Delicious food, served with mountains of bread, and inexpensive.

Demircioğlu Caddesi
0286 217 7257
8am–9pm

Yalova (££)

The seafront in Çanakkale is lined with restaurants, but few of them are worth bothering about. This fish restaurant near the ferry port, is undoubtedly the pick of the bunch. A rooftop terrace and fine views are added attractions.

Gümrük Sok, Liman Caddesi
0286 217 1045 **Lunch, dinner**

Çeşme

Chefs Palace (££)

Brightly lit at night, the restaurant is easy to find in the middle of town near the sea. The speciality is Mediterranean cuisine but there are also Turkish dishes and a selection of vegetarian choices.

Sakarya Mh Memis S. 10
0232 712 8150 **8.30am–10.30pm, summer only**

Dost Pide & Pizza (£–££)
A bright and cheerful tourist restaurant in Ilıca, 4km (2.5 miles) west of Çeşme, with tables filling the pavement. As well as the pizzas, there is also a variety of meat dishes on the menu.
İifne Caddesi, Ilıca
0232 723 2059
8am–late
***Dolmuş* to Çeşme**

Sahíl (£–££)
This is a typical Çeşme restaurant facing the sea, with indoor and outdoor tables, and a menu that has both Turkish and European dishes, including kebabs and pizza. The Sahíl was established in 1954, and is one of the oldest restaurants catering for visitors.
Cumhuriyet Meydanı 13
0232 712 8294
8am–11pm

İzmir

Le Chalet (££)
The street Le Chalet is on is the continuation of the street market behind the Hilton Hotel. There are tables indoor and out, and the menu includes grills, casseroles, salads, pasta and Turkish pitta bread.
1375 Sokak 0232 422 2888 8.30am–10pm
61–3, 110, 112, 116, 150

Chinese Restaurant (££)
Situated down a street behind the Hilton Hotel, this licensed restaurant has a long menu of beef, chicken, duck, seafood, rice and noodle dishes. The cook's specials include a hot cabbage salad, lamb with green onion, fried chicken with orange sauce and steamed dumplings. Take-away service available.
1379 Sokak 0232 483 0079 Lunch and dinner
62, 68, 77

Deniz (££–£££)
The Deniz specializes in fish dishes, and is regarded as the best fish restaurant in town. You may need to make a reservation to secure one of the outdoor tables. Popular with business people during the week, less formal at weekends.
Atatürk Caddesi 188-B
0232 422 0601 Lunch and dinner

Fish House (££)
One of a number of restaurants lining the waterfront promenade, this is a coolly calm restaurant with crisp white tablecloths and outside tables in summer. The food, with seafood a specialty, is excellent.
Atatürk Caddesi 174/1-A, Kordon 0232 463 1020
Lunch and dinner

Seçkin (£)
In the centre of town, with a good choice of Turkish pizzas, grills and pastries, and an upstairs area with half a dozen computers and access to e-mail and the Internet, paid for by the half-hour.
M Kemalettin Caddesi 16/A, Konak 0232 489 2404
8am–late Several

Window on the Bay (£££)
Open nightly, except Sunday, the Window on the Bay is on the 31st floor of the Hilton Hotel. Nowhere in town offers finer views of the city. An international menu is accompanied by

Turkish (Vegetarian) Delight
Vegetarian options are a bit limited, but possible with cold *meze* providing an excellent if somewhat samey meal. Try a light lunch of salad with excellent brown breads, based on Turkish village recipes, or a breakfast of goma wheat served with *gomassio* (sesame seed and rock salt roasted together and pounded to a paste), oregano and olives. Vegetarian pizza is usually available in pizza restaurants.

Gender Rules

Once off the beaten tourist track, women travellers may find themselves being ushered into a separate room in a restaurant, or placed in a corner as far away from the male customers as possible. This is the way things are in Turkey and it would be considered very rude to create a fuss. In the resort areas, on the other hand, separation of the sexes has long been forgotten.

piano music until 10pm, and then a band takes over.

Gaziosmanpasa Bulvarı, İzmir 0232 441 6060 7pm–2am 61–3, 110, 112, 116, 150

Kuşadası

Captain's House Restaurant (££)

Next door to the pub of the same name, this is a comfortable place to enjoy seafood, international dishes and good Turkish *meze*. Photographs and charts relating to the Turkish navy decorate the walls and just about any other available space.

Istikal 0256 614 4754 8.30am–late

Ferah Balik Restaurant (££)

Right beside the sea, near the fishing harbour, this is a charmingly laid back restaurant with excellent seafood, a seafront terrace in summer and fine views of Bird Island.

İskele Yanı 0256 614 1281 Lunch, dinner

Gondolen Pizzeria (£)

Small, modern, licensed café with a large menu of over 20 pizzas to choose from as well as other possibilities, including English-style breakfast and a children's menu. A few doors up on the same side of the street, opposite the Otel Atadan, there is a less expensive, unlicensed *pide* (pizza) café specialising in the one dish: a tasty mixed *pide*, with or without meat, accompanied by a Turkish yogurt.

Ismet Inönö Bulvarı 19 0256 614 5417 8am–late

Güldüoğlu (££–£££)

In the centre of town, close to Beer Street, this is an elegant, air-conditioned restaurant with rosewood furniture and modern art by the painter/proprietor adorning the walls, which is for sale. Mixed menu—grills and pasta dishes—in English, Dutch, French, German and Spanish. Some tables outside.

1/C Zabita Amirliğ, Alti 0256 614 8637 8am–11pm Free transport to/from hotels

Holiday Inn (£)

In the heart of Kuşadası, and with a wide-ranging menu designed to appeal to overseas visitors: salads, lasagne, kebabs, moussaka, chicken Kiev, roast beef, steaks, fish and chips, Wiener Schnitzel etc. Stick with the home-made kebabs and you won't be disappointed.

Kahramanlar Caddesi 57/5 0256 612 8940 8am–midnight Free transport to/from hotels

Odin Restaurant (££–£££)

A left turn at the bottom of Barbaros Hayrettin Street as you face the sea brings you to Odin's Restaurant, on the left. It looks out across the sea and there are outdoor tables and a large menu of seafood and meat dishes. It's popular with holiday-makers and is open until late.

Güvercinada Caddesi 0256 614 4934 8am–1am

Sultan Han (£££)

A charming setting in the old part of town; the Sultan Han

is in a renovated old caravanserai and some care has been taken to retain a traditional atmosphere. The menu is fairly wide ranging, but the Turkish dishes are definitely the ones to go for. The *meze* are very tasty and there is a good selection of traditional sugary Turkish desserts. Belly dancers sometimes provide live entertainment.

Bahar Sokak 8
0256 614 6380/3849
Lunch, dinner

Yucca Restaurant (££)

Large, very commercial tented restaurant serving almost every cuisine under the sun, from Mexican, Indian and Chinese to French and Italian—and Turkish, of course. With a shady garden terrance and lively atmosphere and good food, it's the hangout choice for locals.

Soğlik **0256 612 0769**
Lunch, dinner May–Oct

Selçuk

Kalenin Prensin (££)

Attractive gardens, a shaded terrace and an ancient Roman menu alongside the standard Turkish fare to get you in the mood for visiting Ephesus all help to make this one of the more unusual and entertaining restaurants in the area.

İsabey Mahallesi Eski İzmir
0232 892 2087
Lunch, dinner May–Oct

Özdamar (£)

The pedestrianized street that begins at the Artemis fountain has a number of almost identical restaurants: this is the one nearest to the fountain. A multilingual menu (English, Flemish, French, Italian and German) features mostly grills, pizzas and salads. Outdoor tables and long hours.

Cengiz Topel Caddesi 65
0232 891 4097
7.30am–midnight

Pink Bistro (£)

The menu here includes hamburgers, spaghetti, kebabs, Turkish pizza and salads. It is not gourmet dining, but it is pleasant enough. Late at night this is a lively bar playing taped music to a European clientele in the 20–30 age group.

Atatürk Mh Saigburg Sokak
0232 891 4015
9am–2.30am

Seçkin (££)

The food is well presented and the service is pleasantly unobtrusive in this terrace restaurant on the pedestrianized Çengiz Topel Caddesi.

Çengiz Topel Caddesi
0232 892 6698
Lunch, dinner

Selçuk Köftecisi (£–££)

With a reputation among locals as the best place in town for *köfte* (meatballs), this restaurant now occupies a larger space on the road near the bus station, behind the tourist office. Try the *köfte* with a salad and a choice of kebabs, a glass of *raki* and to round off one of the sweet desserts to complete your meal.

Cahabettin Dede Caddesi
0232 892 6696
Summer 7.30am–11pm; winter 7.30am–9pm

Fresh Fish

Fresh fish caught locally is one of the delights of Turkey. The price may vary according to weight and the market. Sardines (*sardalya*), grey mullet (*kefal*) and black bream (*sangöz*) are usually the least expensive but it is worth spending more for seabass (*levrek*), turbot (*kalkan*) and gilt-head bream (*çipura*).

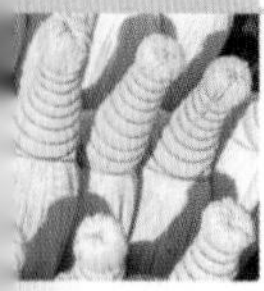

Southern Aegean

Tex-Mex in Turkey
Bodrum is a surprising place to find good Tex-Mex food, but if you are seeking an alternative to the standard tourist menu, the Picante restaurant serves *nachos* and *tacos* for starters and *tapas* including aubergine and parmigiana slices, shrimps baked in artichoke with béchamel sauce, or corn tortilla soup. *Fajitas* come in fish, meat and vegetarian forms, and black-eyed chicken is another favourite.

Bitez Beach

Istanbul Restaurant (££–£££)

Hard to miss on the beach pathway, this place brings food from an extensive menu to your umbrella-shaded table. Turkish music at night and frozen strawberry margaritas for an aperitif.

Bitez Beach ☎ 0252 363 7230 Lunch, dinner Free transport to/from hotels

Bodrum

Antique Theatre Restaurant (£££)

Situated opposite the ancient theatre, this is one of the most prestigious restaurants in Bodrum. Seafood is a speciality, but international dishes such as duck with caramalized oranges, also feature on the menu. Torch-lit poolside setting, with illuminated views of the Castle of St Peter at night.

Kibris Sehitlehri Caddesi ☎ 0252 316 6053 Dinner only in summer *Dolmuş*/minibus to Bodrum

Buğday (££)

Excellent vegetarian restaurant using fresh local produce. The lack of alcohol is made up for by the freshly squeezed fruit juices. Natural products from olive oil to soap are also on sale.

Türkuyusu Caddesi ☎ 0252 316 2969 Lunch, dinner all year *Dolmuş*/minibus to Bodrum

Cavallino (££)

Italian-style restaurant in the Günden Resort Hotel at the west end of town. It overlooks the pool, and the food tastes authentically Italian. Also a good wine list.

Günden Resort Hotel, Gümbet ☎ 0252 313 4382 Lunch, dinner, summer only *Dolmuş*/minibus to Bodrum

The Difference (££)

The Dutch chef and proprietor brings a touch of European *élan* to the menu. The excellent home-made soups are tasty, and the steaks are well above the usual standard.

Narrow street running from Atatürk Caddesi to the sea ☎ 0252 316 8396 Lunch, dinner, summer only

Epsilon (£££)

Turkish and Mediterranean cuisine in a delightful restaurant tucked away down an alley, but well worth seeking out. There's a romantic atmosphere at the garden tables, good food at reasonable prices and a peaceful and relaxing ambience in general. Some dishes available for vegetarians.

Turgutreis Caddesi ☎ 0252 313 2964 Dinner only *Dolmuş*/minibus to Bodrum

The Han (££)

The food is an unoriginal mixture of Turkish and international dishes, but the location is more unusual—in a renovated *han*—an Ottoman inn—and there is the bonus of live evening entertainment. Oriental dancers warm up the atmosphere, and customers who have drunk enough *raki* are tempted to try out a belly dance or two, to the accompaniment of drums and flutes.

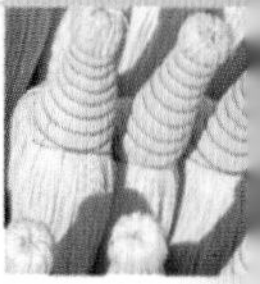

Kale Sokak 0252 316 7951/316 1615 Lunch, dinner *Dolmuş*/minibus to Bodrum

Kocadon (£££)

This is the way one would like all of Bodrum to look; the restaurant is set among ancient-looking stone walls and houses enclosing a quiet courtyard with a small pool in a garden. Sparkling white linen on the tables, jazz or classical music in the background, and good Turkish cuisine add to the air of romance. Make a reservation and arrive in time to enjoy a cocktail by the poolside and soak up the atmosphere.

Neyzen Tevfik Caddesi 160
0252 614 63705
8pm–midnight
***Dolmuş*/minibus to Bodrum**

La Jolla Bistro (££–£££)

Full to bursting with eager drinkers in summer, out of season this is a delightful little wine bar and bistro on the seafront, with mouthwatering French-style cuisine food. Extensive wine list and nice cocktails. Also a branch in the Xuma Beach Club, Yalıkavak from June to September.

Neyzin Tevfik Caddesi 174, Karada Marina Karşısı 0252 313 7660 Lunch, dinner all year *Dolmuş*/minibus to Bodrum

Marina Yacht Club (££–£££)

There's more than one restaurant in this well-run complex, with live music every night. Locals like this place and with good reason, it's got a laid-back atmosphere, good seafood and friendly staff.

Neyzen Tevfik Caddesi 0252 316 1228 Lunch, dinner *Dolmuş*/minibus to Bodrum

Nur (££)

An elegant Mediterranean setting is successfully evoked in the courtyard of this townhouse. The menu is not large and the portions not huge, but there is a good selection of fish and meat dishes, and the atmosphere of the place compensates.

Cumhuriyet Caddesi, Eski Adilye Sokak 5 0252 313 1065 Lunch and dinner
***Dolmuş*/minibus to Bodrum**

Picante (££–£££)

Tex-Mex food (► 96, panel) is served in this very popular and chic restaurant, not easy to find in one of the quieter corners of Bodrum (► 60). Nice little wine bar for pre-dinner drinks; the wine list includes imported wines. Outdoor tables at the back.

Türkkuyusu Mah Kğlcu Sokak 8 0252 316 0270
8am–2.30pm

The Secret Garden (£££)

The food here is Mediterranean and includes frogs' legs in garlic, chicken and sage ravioli, seafood soup with vermouth, tomato and pesto tart and tapenade—and that's just the starters! Main dishes include slow-cooked lamb with aubergine, filet steak with spinach and rosti, seabass and olive potatoes – you get the picture. It's basically some of the best food to be found on the Turkish west coast.

Eskicesme Mah Danaci Sokak 20 0252 313 1641
Dinner only, summer only
***Dolmuş*/minibus to Bodrum**

Meze

Often translated as appetizers or hors d'oeuvres, Turkish *meze* are neither of those things. Vegetarians can make a full meal out of three or four on a plate accompanied with rice and bread. A full-scale Turkish meal starts with a selection of cold, then hot *meze* and by the time the main course arrives the appetite can be flagging. Especially filling are the green peppers stuffed with rice, nuts and currants, and cooked in olive oil.

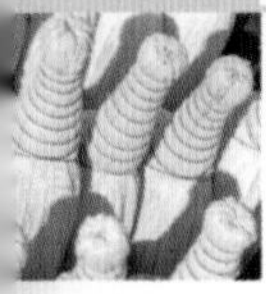

Raki
The national alcohol drink is distilled from grape juice and flavoured with aniseed. It is usually mixed with water, whereupon it becomes cloudy, and is taken with meals. The high alcohol content, over 40 per cent, may explain why it is not so popular as an aperitif, because it certainly packs a punch on an empty stomach. Try it with some cheese and watermelon.

Fethiye

Birlik (£)
Adjacent to the Mara Hotel, and a few doors down from the cinema, this self-service restaurant offers tasty and inexpensive lokanta-style meals with mountains of bread.
Kral Sokak 10 0252 614 2145 Lunch, dinner

Marina Lokantası (££)
Formerly known as Rafet, this is one of Fethiye's oldest and best restaurants, specializing in seafood, perfectly sited on the promenade by the fishing harbour.
Kordon Boyu 0252 614 1106 Lunch, dinner

Meğri (£)
A well-established restaurant that has acquired a good reputation for its authentic Turkish meals. To order, just point to the dish you want. There is a second Meğri restaurant in Çarşı Caddesi.
Eski Cami Gecidi Likya Sokak 8 0252 614 4046 Lunch, dinner

Göcek

Göcek (£–££)
Göcek, on the main coast road between Fethiye and Köyceğiz, attracts travellers passing through with their own transport, and also yachting customers, who tend to push the prices up a little. The fresh fish is tempting, though, and the surrounding landscape makes a peaceful setting.
Yat Club House 0252 645 1414 Lunch, dinner *Dolmuş*/minibus to/from Fethiye and Köyceğiz

Gümüşlük

Gümüş Café (££)
Situated at the quieter end of the beach, this is a restaurant where you can drop in at breakfast or lunchtime for delicious home-made bread, or enjoy an evening casserole—it's all in a lovely romantic setting.
Gümüşluk 0252 394 4234 8am–late

İçmeler

Kerem (££)
A traditional Turkish menu is offered here, featuring favourites such as steamed lamb shin and kebabs. What adds to the pleasure of dining here is the style of the building, designed by a famous architect—ask the owners for details.
Osmangazi 24 0252 455 4869 Lunch, dinner

Kalkan

Belgin's Kitchen (££–£££)
This is a well-established restaurant evoking Ottoman times, with the help of plush cushions on the floor. Superb food on the menu with specialities such as *mantı* (Turkish ravioli).
Yaliboyu, 1 Kalkan 0242 844 3614; fax 844 3437 6pm–10pm

Bezigran Kitchen (£)
The family does all the cooking and bread-baking here. Everything is traditional and tasty and cooked fresh to order. There are pretty tables outside in summer for a pleasant eating experience.
Yaliboyu Mahallessi, 1 Kalkan 0242 844 2106 Lunch, dinner

Marmaris

Antique Café (£££)

The location, on the first-floor balcony of the Nestel Marina, gives the Antique an edge over restaurants with lesser views. The food is excellent; great salads.

Nestel Marina 0252 413 2955 8am–late

Pineapple (££)

Another restaurant in the Nestel Marina, this one is on the ground floor, and residents of Marmaris rate it as one of the best half dozen in the town. International cuisine, in a pastoral setting.

Nestel Marina 0252 412 0976 8am–midnight

Portofino (££)

Recommended for its choice of Turkish and British food at reasonable prices. It's a family-oriented, friendly establishment, but beware that it does have satellite sports on a large-screen TV.

Cildir Mah Sokak 164
0252 413 2261
8.30am–late

Rovers Return (£)

In a pleasant garden setting near the sea. Suitable for families with young children who like sausage and chips, omelettes and other British favourites of that sort.

Behind the Atlas Hotel, Kemel El 8am–9pm

Ölüdeniz

Beyaz Yunus (White Dolphin) (£££)

With a fabulous setting overlooking the eastern end of Ölüdeniz beach, a Mediterranean garden and superb food, including seafood specials, this is the place to go for a celebratory night out, or just to enjoy the best this area has to offer.

Ölüdeniz beach 0252 617 0068 Lunch, dinner May–Oct *Dolmuş*/minibus from Fethiye

Kaya Wine House (££)

This renovated stone cottage with a lovely garden in the ghost village serves memorable meals and some reasonable house wine, with stews, roasts and summer barbecues. The perfect place for a relaxing lunch or pleasant dinner.

Gökçeburun Mahallesi No. 70, Keçiler 0252 618 0454/612 0476 Lunch, dinner *Dolmuş*/minibus to from Fethiye

Restaurant La Turquoise (££)

A poolside restaurant for the Montana Pine Resort Hotel that serves international cuisine. The pleasant setting and the live classical Turkish music contribute to the ambience of fine dining at a reasonable price.

Montana Pine Resort, Ölüdeniz 0252 616 6366
Lunch, dinner
***Dolmuş*/minibus from Fethiye**

Yalıkavak

Ali Baba (££)

Overlooking the harbour, this is an ideal spot to enjoy home-made *meze*, with fish and steaks for a main course. *Pide* bread is cooked here in a traditional oven.

Seafront 0252 385 4063
Lunch and dinner
***Dolmuş*/minibus to/from Bodrum**

Pastries and Puddings

Pastry shops are called *pastahanes*. For sheer sugary, gooey indulgence there is nothing to beat a typical Turkish pastry, soaked in rich oil and filled with cream or syrup. Turkish puddings are just as sweet and also pose a challenge to anyone watching their weight. The most famous confectionery in the world, *lokum* (Turkish delight), is made from solidified sugar and pectin, flavoured with rosewater and sprinkled with icing sugar.

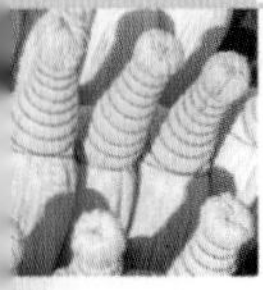

Northern Aegean

Prices

The **£** symbol represents pproximate prices per room per night, regardless of single or double occupancy. Because of the former uncertainty over currency fluctuations hotels usually quote prices in US dollars.

£ = US$30–50
££ = US$50–90
£££ = over US$90

Assos

Assos Kervansaray (££)
One of several small hotels in Behremkale, below Assos, this is a charming stone building, with fine sea views, a pool and good restaurant with an outdoor terrace. Boat trips and watersports also available.
Behramkale, Ayvacik
0286 721 7093/7199; fax 0286 721 7200; www.assos kervansaray.com

Çanakkale

Akol (££–£££)
This 4-star hotel at the east end of town is the most comfortable accommodation base for visits to Troy and Gallipoli. The two blocks have a small pool between them. Most of the 136 rooms face the Dardanelles, and there are two restaurants and a roof bar.
Kordonboyu **0286 217 9456; fax 0286 217 2897; www.hotelakol.com.tr**

Anzac House (£)
Good budget choice. The single, double and dormitory rooms are clean. Facilities include an inexpensive cafeteria, laundry service, internet, summer barbecues and hot showers. Member of the Turkish Youth Hostels Association.
Cumhuriyet Meydanı 61
0286 213 5969; fax 0286 217 2906; www.anzachouse.com

Çesme

Sheraton Çesme (£££)
A seriously luxurious 5-star resort, about 2km (1 mile) from the centre of town, with a private beach, several restaurants, superb food, a rooftop bar, indoor and outdoor pools and a sybaritic spa.
Sifme Caddesi 35, Ilıca
0232 723 1240; www.sheratoncesme.com

Gökçeada

Barba Yorgo (£–££)
Rooms at a taverna on the island west of Çanakkale. A Greek atmosphere enlivens the place considerably. Close to beaches and footpaths.
Gökçeada **0286 887 4247; www.barbayorgo.com**
By boat from Çanakkale

Herakleıa

Agora (£)
One of the most pleasant places for an overnight stay amidst the evocative remains of ancient Herakleıa (the modern village name is Kapıkırı). Simple pine beds, a pleasant veranda and lots of local information. No English but German is spoken.
Kapıkırı **0252 543 5445; fax 0252 543 5567** ***Dolmuş*/minibus from Çamiçi or by boat from south shore of Lake Bafa**

İzmir

Antik Han Hotel (£)
One of the city's few 'special' hotels, in a restored historic shopping mall in the middle of the market area. It has a lobby bar, restaurant and shady courtyard garden, a good place to sit out of the heat of the day or escape the bustle beyond the doors. Rooms are unpretentious but then, so is the price.
Anafartalar Caddesi 600, Mezarlikbası **0232 489 2750; fax 0232 483 5925; www.otelantikham.com**

Kismet (££)
A comfortable friendly mid-range hotel conveniently set in a quiet side street a couple of blocks walk from the seafront. The rooms and public areas are pleasant if not inspired and have all the facilities you need. The restaurant is a little dark but the food is good.
✉ 1377 Sok 9 ☎ 0232 463 3850; fax 0232 421 4856; email kismet@efes.met.tr

Kuşadası

Atinç Otel (££)
Perfectly situated on the seafront, a few minutes' walk from the town centre, the Antiç is a modern 4-star hotel with great sea views, a bar, two good restaurants (one a popular pizzeria) and a rooftop pool. The rooms, which have balconies, are comfortable and the staff are friendly and helpful.
✉ Atatürk Bulvarı ☎ 0256 614 7608; fax 0232 614 4967; www.atincotel.com

Liman Hotel (£)
Around the corner from the tourist office, the best rooms at the Liman have balconies and face the sea. All rooms have air-conditioning and breakfast is served on the roof. Other facilities include laundry service, internet, restaurant and bar.
✉ Buyral Road ☎ 0256 614 7770; fax 0256 614 6913; www.kushadasihotels.com/liman

Villa Konak (£–££)
A welcoming 'special' hotel, in a restored mansion in a hilly residential area of the town. The rooms are simply but elegantly furnished. The excellent meals are taken family-style at a huge communal table, the shady courtyard garden is ideal for to relax in, and there are regular parties at night.
✉ Yildirim Caddesi 55 ☎ 0256 614 6318; fax 0256 614 1524; www.villakonakhotel.com

Manisa

Anemon Manisa (£££)
A couple of kilometres outside Manisa, on the road to İzmir, a mountain provides a dramatic backdrop to the hotel's location. Indoor and outdoor swimming pools, tennis courts and a fitness centre all invite you to extend your stay here.
✉ Manisa ☎ 0232 233 4141; fax 0232 233 4595; www.anemonhotels.com

Selçuk

Kalehan (££)
The Ottoman charm of the Kalehan puts it in a class of its own. Near the castle, on the main road through town, the rooms are delightfully furnished and comfortably modern. Antiques and artefacts are everywhere and lend character to the place. There is a swimming pool and a good restaurant.
✉ Atäturk Caddesi 49 ☎ 0232 892 6154; fax 0232 892 2169; www.kalehan.com

Kirkinca Konaklari (£)
Set in the pretty village of Sirince 9km (5.5 miles) from Selçuk, combine the calm of the countryside, traditional Turkish village life and sightseeing in Selçuk and Ephesus. Antiques and modern conveniences blend.
✉ Sirince ☎ 0232 898 3133; www.kirkinca.com

Looking for a Room
If you are travelling around you should be able to find rooms on the spot, except in the more popular resorts of Kuşadası, Bodrum and Marmaris. In these places it is best to ask the tourist office for help. If travelling by public transport in summer, you are likely to be approached by touts at the station, but, unless you are desperate, you should reject their offers of help. They can be unreliable, and will expect a commission from the proprietor, who will add it to your bill.

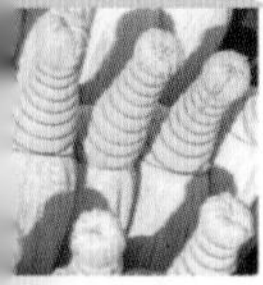

Southern Aegean

Pansiyons
For an inexpensive night's lodging, look for a *pansiyon* (pension) sign. A *pansiyon* is a cross between a bed and breakfast and a small guesthouse, and is typically a friendly and welcoming place. Rooms tend to be plain but clean and the better ones will have their own toilet and shower. Hot water and some kind of laundry facility is usually provided, and breakfast is always available, but may cost extra.

Bodrum

Durak (£)
This is a relatively quiet little *pansiyon*, notwithstanding its position at the Halikarnas Disco end of town. A neat little front garden and terrace adds to the charm. All rooms have their own toilet and shower and some also have a small balcony. The Uğur (☎ 0252 316 2106), next door, is also worth trying if Durak is full.
✉ Rasathane Sokak 8
☎ 0252 316 1564

Karia Princess (£££)
This award-winning hotel is the classiest place to stay in Bodrum. It is a little way to the west of the town centre and consequently not plagued by disco music all night long. There is, however, a neat little cinema near by and the largest supermarket to be found in any of the resort towns along the coast. The hotel's Turkish bath is a superb recreation of an Ottoman-style *hamam*. Most rooms have a pleasant balcony, and the 20 per cent that don't are less expensive.
✉ Canli Dere Sokak 15
☎ 0252 316 8971; fax 0252 316 8979; www.kariaprincess.com

Majesty Hotel Marina (££)
This comfortably elegant little 4-star hotel right opposite the Marina on the Bodrum seafront is just far enough away from the party zone to be relatively quiet, but easily close enough to walk to the sights. Pool, restaurant and well-appointed rooms.
✉ Neyzen Tevfik Caddesi 222
☎ 0252 316 2260 fax 0252 316 2347; www.majestyresorts.com

Su Hotel (£££)
There are at present ten air-conditioned rooms here, although there are plans for expansion. Cheerful decor greets you, along with a pool, bar, and fruit trees all around. It's a pretty cool place to stay.
✉ Turguteris ☎ 0252 316 6906; fax 0252 316 7391; www.suhotel.net

Datça

Dede Pansiyon (£)
Some 3km (2 miles) from Datça, this *pansiyon* is about six rooms with kitchen in a stone dwelling in a lovely rustic setting. It's a great place to stay when the day tours have left and you have the place to yourself. Check out the 1950s fridge by the poolside bar.
✉ Eski Datça ☎ and fax 0256 712 3951

Fethiye and Ölüdeniz

Mara Hotel (£)
Excellent value for money in this friendly and well-run hotel. Facilities include a restaurant, bar, free Internet access, central location and rooms with air-conditioning.
✉ Yah Sokak 2, Fethiye ☎ 0252 614 6722; fax 0252 614 8039

Meri (£££)
This is the place to soak up the sun at Ölüdeniz, and the only hotel inside the designated national park area. There are 75 rooms, a restaurant and garden bar, a playground area for children and laundry. All the usual water-based activities can be arranged here, including diving. Lift service to the beach.

Ölüdeniz 0252 617 0001; fax 0252 617 0010; www.hotelmeri.com
***Dolmuş*/minibus to Fethiye**

Montana Pine Resort (£££)
Set among the forests above Ölüdeniz, with stunning lagoon views, the resort has spacious rooms with balconies, restaurants, bars, a health club and three pools. Shuttle bus to the beach.
Ölüdeniz 0252 616 7108/6366; fax 0252 616 6451; www.montanapine.com
Apr–Oct

İçmeler

Aqua (£££)
Pleasantly landscaped, with palm trees and a garden leading down to the beach. The amenities of İçmeler are within walking distance. The 240 rooms have balconies with partial sea views. Suitable for families; adults can use the fitness centre, gym and tennis court.
İçmeler 0252 455 3633; fax 0252 455 3650 *Dolmuş*/minibus from/to Marmaris

Munamar Vista (£££)
About half of the rooms have a sea view. The hotel backs on to the beach; and the water *dolmuş* from Marmaris makes its final stop here. Turkish bath, pool, fitness centre and large rooms.
Kayabal Caddesi 0252 455 3360; fax 0252 455 3359
***Dolmuş*/minibus and water *dolmuş*, from Marmaris**

Marmaris

Begonya (£)
A cut above the average mid-range hotel in the middle of Marmaris, this is a stone-built house with its own courtyard and characterful architecture. The only disadvantage is the possibility of being kept awake by the nearby pubs.
Hacı Mustafa Sokak 101
0252 412 4095; fax 0252 412 1518

Kaya Maris (££)
Used by some British tour operators, this is a 256-room tourist hotel just 50m from the beach and a half-hour walk from central Marmaris. There is a main pool and a children's pool, Turkish bath, gym, sauna and watersports.
Kenan Evren Bulvarı
0252 413 0233; fax 0252 413 1864; www.hotelkayamaris.com
***Dolmuş*/minibus to/from Marmaris**

Pamukkale

Colossae Hotel Thermal (£££)
One of a positive epidemic of upscale spas that have invaded the plateau behind Pamukkale, the Colossae doubles as a tour-group friendly hotel and health resort. Nicely decorated rooms, gardens, two pools, restaurants and nightclub.
Karahayit 0258 271 4156; fax 0258 271 4250; www.colossae.com.tr

Kervansaray (£)
Cheerful, well-established place in the village at the bottom of the plateau. Clean and friendly with a pool and air-conditioning for summer and central heating for winter. Rooftop restaurant.
Inönü Caddesi, Pamukkale Köyü 0258 272 2209; fax 0258 272 2143; email kervansaray@superonline.com

Resort Hotels
Independent travellers can use the four- and five-star resort hotels, but they are far better value if booked as part of a package deal with a tour operator in your own country. Rooms are usually offered on a bed and breakfast or half-board basis. Families may prefer self-catering, and some of the big resort hotels provide this option. When meals are provided, they are invariably buffets and can become monotonous. Hotels charge extra for drinks at dinner, and some will do so even for a glass of water.

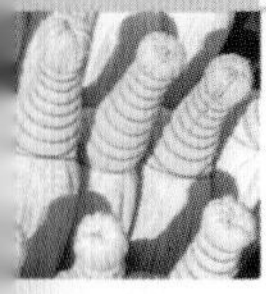

Bazaars

Carpets

Turkish carpets have an international reputation, but there are many differences in quality. Whether a carpet is handwoven or machine-made is fundamental to its value; other things that matter are the density of the knots in handwoven carpets, whether the dyes are either natural or less expensive chemical ones, and whether the carpet is made of wools or silk. The flat-woven, double-sided mats known as *kilims* are always less expensive.

Kuşadası, Bodrum and Marmaris

The big resort towns of Kuşadası, Bodrum and Marmaris all have bazaars (*basar* in Turkish). They are not really the genuine Ottoman emporia that still survive in their medieval forms in Istanbul, and to a lesser extent in İzmir. They are still great places to shop, however, and are based around the traditional shopping areas of town.

Resort bazaars consist of small shops on either side of a pedestrianized street or passageway, many with awnings over their street displays of merchandise. The advantage for the consumer is a high density of tourist-oriented shops, all competing with one another, and the cool shade of the awnings can be a welcome relief in the high season. The drawback is that the constant importuning by proprietors, and roaming touts can become tiresome, especially when you just want to be left alone to consider a purchase. The sales line usually begins with an offer of tea, but bear in mind that such hospitality comes naturally to Turkish people and no commitment is being sought when the offer is made.

The merchandise covers a wide range, especially in Marmaris where boatloads of visitors from Greece arrive daily with Turkish money to spend. Shops selling leather clothing and goods—handbags, travel bags, briefcases, accessories—are all over the place, closely followed by stores selling carpets and *kilims*, jewellery, Meerschaum pipes, ceramics and crafts.

It is worth checking out some of the clothes stores with familiar branded North American and European labels, for these are usually made under licence in Turkey and are consequently often much less expensive than back home. The least expensive items in a bazaar will usually be souvenirs, synthetic apple tea powder, sandals and beachwear, Turkish delight (*lokum*) and other types of confectionery.

İzmir

The maze of narrow streets and cul-de-sacs to the north of Konak Square that make up the city's bazaar date from before the fire of 1922 (➤ 31). There are a number of restored 18th-century caravanserai (where the trading caravans from the East would rest) and a few mosques, including the Hisar Mosque from 1597. This is both the oldest and the largest mosque in İzmir. It's quite easy to get lost in the bazaar so try and check where you are going (see guided walk, ➤ 33).

The countless shops, stalls and workshops are used by Turks rather than tourists, and the clothes and shoe shops are well worth looking into, as are the music shops where the traditional folk music scene flourishes. The atmosphere is the main attraction: it is a place of great interest and character and still the best place to immerse yourself in the sounds, sights and smells of Turkish culture. Don't go on a Sunday, when most of the shops are closed.

Traditional Crafts & Souvenirs

Antiques

Northern Aegean

Bodrum

Ifos
There are two floors in this shop, the upper level devoted to old *kilims* and small carpets, the ground floor crammed full with a miscellany of objects. Not everything is a genuine antique, nor is it claimed to be, and there is a lot to see: this is a good shop to look around when you are not in a hurry. The collection of *hookahs*, old and contemporary, is definitely one of the highlights.
✉ Çarşi Mahallesı Çarşi Içı 6, Sokak 16 ☎ 0252 316 4961 ⏲ 9am–midnight

Southern Aegean

Marmaris

Ottoman
Silver jewellery, clocks, pocket watches, copper utensils, hand embroidery and other items—part of the pleasure of this shop is its chaotic-looking arrangement. It is a serious shop, though with genuine antiques, and shipping can be arranged. Inland, near the bazaar.
✉ Çeşme Mey Grand Pazar 1 ☎ 0252 412 5911 ⏲ 9am–10pm

Arts & Crafts

Northern Aegean

Bodrum

Dalyancı
One of the better shops for gifts, craft and souvenirs. Glass and ceramics in a variety of forms, all in bright cheerful designs and colours, are on display, with fixed prices—which can come as a relief after all that haggling!
✉ Cumhuriyet Caddesi, Alim Bey Pasaji 55 ☎ 0252 313 0214 ⏲ 8.30am–late

Çeşme

Erdal's
Small gifts and souvenirs: crystal, ceramics, brass and copper, onyx, wood carvings, Meerschaum pipes.
✉ 16 Eylül Mh Gümrük Caddesi 21 ☎ 0232 712 6161 ⏲ 8.30am–9pm 🚌 *Dolmuş*/minibus to İzmir

Kuşadası

Asia Shop 2
Tucked away in a street to the rear of Grand Bazaar and best reached by walking up the street behind the tourist office, this store is worth seeking out if you need to buy a lot of small gifts and souvenirs to fit in your case when you go home. There are two floors crammed with inexpensive bric-à-brac, and the fixed prices mean you can wander around looking and choosing instead of having to haggle.
✉ Kibris Caddesi 4 ☎ 0256 614 1393 ⏲ 7.30am–1am

Çerge
This is one of the more tasteful little shops in Kuşadası, partly because it is not totally dependent on tourist trade. In the winter, Turkish shoppers come here to buy attractive decorative items for their homes, while in summer the shop appeals to visitors looking for

The Evil Eye
The belief that some people are capable of inflicting mental and physical harm through their 'evil eye' has a long history in Turkish culture (► 32). The antidote comes in the form of blue beads attached to pendants, chains and even key-rings. Jewellery shops tend to sell the best-quality versions.

Negotiating Skills
Fixed and marked prices are a rarity along the Turkish Aegean, and some haggling is inevitable. Use your experience and judgement to assess what you are prepared to pay and try to compare prices between stores. As a general rule avoid making an offer (which you can never reduce) until the seller has made at least one reduction on their opening price.

something more than a inexpensive souvenir.
Kemal Ankan Caddesi 16
0256 612 5821
8.30–midnight

Dr. Alim Bey Caddesi
Facing the tourist office, turn to the left, with the mosque on your right, and enter the pedestrianized Dr. Alim Bey Cadessi. The street is full of shops selling leather, clothes, jewellery, shoes and souvenirs. The street eventually reaches the Halikarnas Disco, where the shops are replaced by bars and restaurants.
Dr. Alim Bey Caddesi
8.30–late

Music Box
There's a fair selection of cassettes and CDs here, but the real attraction is the traditional Turkish musical instruments for sale. There are simple flutes (*ney*) that are easy to carry, as well as larger and more delicate instruments.
Yildirim Caddesi 13
0256 614 7522 **9am–1am**

Pearl
At Pearl you'll find elegant Turkish arts and crafts, mostly modern in style and including decorative swords, clocks and jewellery. There are also some paintings framed in boxes, with a three-dimensional effect achieved by the layering of material on the small canvas.
Kemal Arikan Caddesi 2
0256 612 0553
10am–11pm

Priene

Onyx Factory and Shop
The workshop and adjoining store are in the corner of the square where the minibuses arrive and depart. Unless the shop is very busy, someone is usually glad to show you around the workshop and explain the process, from the arrival of the uncut stone to its final polishing. Prices are reasonable, and there is a good selection.
Priene **0256 547 1123** **8am–9pm** ***Dolmuş*/minibus from Söke**

Troy

Ilion Tur
Just outside Troy in the village of Trevfikiye, the usual Troy memorabilia is on sale here. Also on sale are Turkish baggy pants, books on ancient history and assorted souvenirs. The stalls facing the main vehicle ferry dock in the town centre sell the cheapest Troy souvenirs.
Trevfikiye **0286 283 0823** **9am–11pm**

Southern Aegean

Didim (Didyma)/ Altınkum

Gallery Kirşehir
An onyx factory and shop, directly opposite the temple of Apollo, with vases, jars, ashtrays and other assorted items for sale. Potential customers are shown around the factory.
Harabeler Kar, Didyma
0256 811 0306 **8am–9pm**
***Dolmuş*/minibus from Söke**

Marmaris

Nur-Bal
A jar or two of Marmaris honey is a distinctive local

souvenir, and this little shop, in the block behind the post office, has a good selection. The dark-coloured, black-pine honey is one of the local specialities, and the *portakal*, is a light-coloured and very sweet variation.

✉ Fevzi Paça Caddesi 9/C ⌚ 8.30am–10pm

Carpets

Northern Aegean

İzmir

Anatolia
High-quality handwoven carpets and *kilims* are sold here. The selection is not huge but broad enough for anyone seriously thinking of making a purchase. For smaller purchases, expect a discount of at least 15 per cent. For really expensive carpets at least 25 per cent should be taken off the asking price.

✉ 928 Sokak 25 (Hilton Hotel Shopping Mall) ☎ 0232 441 7578 ⌚ Mon–Sat 9–9

Mihrap
Handwoven carpets of silk, wool and cotton and a selection of *kilims*. Bargain hard and expect at least 30 per cent off the asking price. Tucked away in a modern little mall in the bazaar. Look for the Parfümerai shop on a corner along Anafartalar Caddesi—the entrance to the mall is alongside it.

✉ Kapalicarsi, Anafartalar Caddesi, Konak ☎ 0232 484 0425 ⌚ 9am–7pm 🚌 86, 169

Kuşadası

Faberce
This well-established store, easy to find near the entrance to the bazaar, opens early in the morning to catch passengers disembarking from the countless cruise ships that stop in Kuşadası. There are two floors of carpets and *kilims*, and the courteous staff don't go in for the hard sell—they are quite persuasive though. Delivery and insurance is arranged for bulky purchases, usually around 2 per cent of the price.

✉ Söförler Sokak 3, Grand Bazaar ☎ 0256 614 8885 ⌚ 7.30am–midnight

Selçuk

Nomadic Art Gallery
Come here for expensive, hand-woven wool carpets from Anatolia, less expensive cotton ones and also imports from Iran and Afghanistan. You'll receive the usual cup of tea and lots of friendly chat, but in any Selçuk carpet shop it pays to know something about carpets and to be able to distinguish between materials of different quality.

✉ Atatürk Mh Cengiz Topel Caddesi 26/A ☎ 0232 891 8650 ⌚ 8am–11pm

Southern Aegean

Bodrum

Carpets & *Kilims*
Heaps of carpets and above average expertize in the person of Sayın Burku, a man whose workers have produced the world's largest Turish carpet (8.7m x 19.2m/ 29ft x 63ft) for a Kuwaiti sheikh. It took 13 girls 14 months to make. At the time of writing he was in the

Long Hours
Unless otherwise stated, all the shops mentioned here are open seven days a week and never close for lunch. Typical hours are from 8am to 9 or 10pm. In the popular resorts, such as Kuşadası, sales staff will still be asking you what country you come from and offering apple tea at well past midnight.

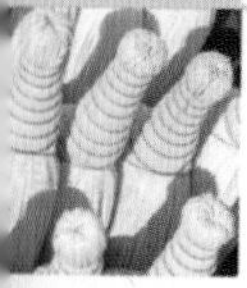

What to Buy?
Apart from the obvious, and more expensive, possibilities—leather, jewellery, carpets and ceramics—consider some of the less heavily touted items available along the coast. Wooden chess boards inlaid with cedar, or heavier onyx ones, are often of good value, as are portable backgammon (*tavla*) sets. Hookahs (*nargiles*) are ornamental; bowls and vases of alabaster are also worth looking out for.

middle of an even bigger one. Smaller offerings for normal homes are readily available.
Neyzen Tevfik Caddesi 40
0252 316 4571; www.sayinburku.com **9am–10pm**

Gallery Mustafa
Ranks with Galleri Anatolia as one of the better carpet and *kilim* shops in Bodrum. If your purchase is too big to carry to your hotel, the shop can arrange safe delivery to your home.
Dr. Alim Ekinici Caddesi 48
0252 313 1043; www.gallerymustafa.com
9am–10pm

Fethiye

Old Orient *Kilim* Bazaar
Two floors of hand-made carpets and *kilims* from all over Turkey. Run by a friendly, soft-sell proprietor who repairs carpets when the tourist season ends. Some souvenirs for sale also.
Karagözler Caddesi 5
0252 612 1059
9am–midnight

Marmaris

Oriental
A self-styled 'carpet palace', this comfortable shop is easy to find, just next to the tourist office facing the sea. It has a reasonable selection of carpets and *kilims*, but you should go knowing something about what you want and the likely price—as in all such stores, the prices are not exactly the same for all customers. Some astute bargaining would not go amiss here.
Yat Limanı 3 **0252 412 4818** **8am–midnight**

Jewellery

Northern Aegean

İzmir

Sevgi Youlu
This is not a shop but a pedestrianized street directly behind the Hilton hotel. At weekends especially, the street is lined on both sides with stalls displaying trays of rings, chains and earrings. There are no marked prices, but this is not a tourist market and prices, arrived at after weighing the merchandise, are very reasonable. Ask for a discount, and expect 10–20 per cent off the asking price.
Sevgi Youlu **9–9**
62, 68, 77

Selçuk

Golden Ephesus Jewellery Centre
A vast jewellery emporium with styles and quality at all prices and enough jewellers on the premises to make up your designs during your stay. Demonstrations of the craft and loose stones for sale.
Aydın Karayolu 3km (2miles), Mersinli Mevkii, Selçuk **0232 892 9550; www.goldenephesus.com**
9am–10pm

Southern Aegean

Bodrum

Galeri Turquoise
Excellent gallery with some unusual and beautiful one-off

designs amidst the more usual offerings.
✉ **Gümüslük Yolu Mevkii** ☎ **0252 394 3818** 🕘 **9am–10pm**

Fethiye

Erol's Gold
This is a large jewellery emporium with precious and semi-precious stones and the whole range of rings, necklaces, bracelets, and wonderful earrings.
✉ **Hamam Sokak 7** ☎ **0252 614 9251/612 2929** 🕘 **9am–10pm**

Mamaris

Vogue Jewellery & Diamond Centre
What it says on the tin, a large emporium glistening with gold and precious stones, plus jewellery made to your own design. They offer a hotel shuttle and will even bring things to your hotel room!
✉ **Kemal Elgin Bulvarı** ☎ **0252 6 413 4875** 🕘 **9am–10pm**

Leather

Northern Aegean

Kuşadası

Albatros
There are lots of places to check prices on and around this street, and Albatros is a good place to start. There are two floors of leather goods: belts, briefcases, backpacks and handbags.
✉ **Barbaros Hayrettin Paşa Street** ☎ **0256 614 1918** 🕘 **9am–late**

Galeri Sultan
Claims to be the oldest leather emporium in Kuşadası. A good collection of jackets and some less expensive waistcoats. A family-run shop with a prime location in the Grand Bazaar.
✉ **Grand Bazaar 5** ☎ **0256 612 4569** 🕘 **7.30am–1am**

Selçuk

Tomurcuk
Situated opposite the Nomadic Art Gallery (► 107), this shop has a good selection of jackets, luggage, belts and other accessories.
✉ **Cengiz Topel Caddesi 27A** ☎ **0232 892 6089** 🕘 **8.30–late**

Southern Aegean

Bodrum

Gazelle Leather & Gift Shop Handicraft
With a bit of a mixture of merchandise, there is a small collection of leather jackets and belts and a whole host of less expensive craft items, such as small inlaid boxes. There are also picture frames, a jewellery section, souvenirs and gifts.
✉ **Neyzen Tefvik Caddesi 124** ☎ **0252 316 9707** 🕘 **9.30am–midnight**

Marmaris

Duygu Bag Shop
A bazaar shop with quality leather travel bags, hand bags, belts and briefcases. There are marked prices on the items but you can still ask for a discount. There is a similar shop at the other end of the pedestrianized passageway, so compare products and prices.
✉ **Tepe Mah Rıhtım Sokak 11/A** ☎ **0252 412 8117** 🕘 **9am–midnight**

Leather Jackets
Do not expect any great bargains: good Turkish leather jackets are not cheap, but they should be still less expensive than jackets of similar quality back home. Spend some time comparing prices and take time trying them on. Check the stitching carefully and be sure to take the jacket out of the shop to check the colour in natural light. You will find a good selection at Tunç Leather in Fethiye (✉ Paspatur Mevkii, Hamam Sokak ☎ 0252 612 3744).

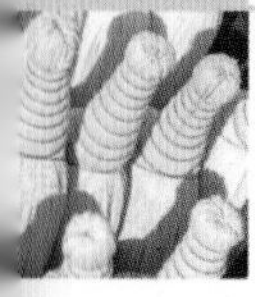

Children's Attractions

The Open Sea
Getting there is half the fun, and a journey across open sea to a Greek island is enjoyable for all ages. Ferries operate between:

Çeşme and Chios
Ayvalık and Lesbos
Kuşadası and Samos
Bodrum and Kos
Bodrum/Marmaris and Rhodes

Turkey does not have many attractions specifically designed for children, but it is a welcoming place for them all the same. Turks are usually quite happy to see children at shops and restaurants.

Most of the better resort hotels will have a children's pool separate from the main pool. Some hotels, usually in co-operation with a tour operator in your own country, have special clubs for children (3- to 6 year-olds and 7- to 12 year-olds)—effectively taking them off your hands for morning and afternoon sessions. Baby-sitting in the evening is not very easy to arrange.

Beaches

Western Turkey has plenty of beaches for young children who are happy to build sandcastles and play under supervision in shallow water. It can sometimes be difficult to find shady places on the sand, though, so remember hats, sunblock and other protection from the sun. Always check with your hotel and the local tourist office about the advisability of swimming off the local beach: don't assume that just because parasols and deckchairs line the sand the sea must be safe. Apart from undertows and difficult currents, some stretches of sea are sometimes just too polluted to be healthy. The beaches at Calış (➤ 64) and Turgetreis (➤ 89) are safe in so far as the sea there is shallow for a long way out. This is also true of the beach at İstuzu (Dalyan ➤ 65), which is a nesting site for loggerhead turtles.

Parks

Kültürpark, İzmir
This is the main park in İzmir and is home to a zoo and amusement park as well as a restaurant and quiet gardens. It is also the site of the İzmir International Fair, but for most of the year it's a welcome oasis in the centre of the city.

Waterparks

Aquapark Dedeman
There are waterslides and pools at this fun waterpark next to the Dedeman Hotel, 3km (2 miles) from Bodrum town centre. For adults there are bars and restaurants in the hotel.
✉ Dedeman Hotel, Turguteris Yölü ☎ 0252 358 5950 🕐 9am–10pm

Atlantis Aquapark & Aquapark İçmeler
The Atlantis Aquapark is a water-based fun park for children. Warerslides and a 'froggy island'.There is a bar for parents. Aquapark Içmeler, under the same management as Atlantis, is on the right as you enter İçmeler from Marmaris.
Atlantis Aquapark
✉ Marmaris ☎ 0252 413 0308 🕐 Morning to evening
Aquapark İçmeler
☎ 0252 455 5049 🕐 Morning to evening

Aquafantasy, Kusadası
A 5-star beach hotel with an elaborate aquapark, also open to day visitors.
✉ Ephesus Beach, Pamucak, between Kusadası and Selçuk ☎ 0233 893 1111, www.aquafantasy.com 🕐 Daily Apr–Oct

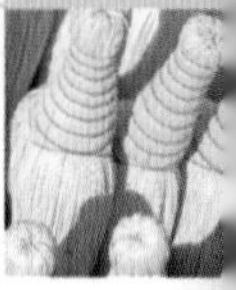

Activities

Cinema (➤ panel)

Karia Princess Cinema

This is the neatest little cinema on the Turkish Aegean coast. It's in the bottom floor of a hotel in Bodrum, and has a small bar serving drinks and confectionery. Come the obligatory intermission everyone still rushes out for a cigarette. Curious but cute.

✉ Canli Dere Sokak 15, Bodrum ☎ 0252 316 6272 ⌚ Afternoon, evening and night shows

Horse-riding

Horse Safari & Horse Camp

A way for older children and adults to see the landscape from a different point of view. Bodrum's Horse Camp offers individual riding lessons, 1- to 2-hour trips and overnight trekking. Available through all local travel agents.

Hills Tour ✉ Atatürk Bulvarı 70, Kuşadası ☎ 0256 612 8332
Horse Camp ✉ Bitez Beach ☎ 0252 614 31961

Walking

Although most of the serious walking in Turkey is done in the central mountains, this can still be a rewarding activity in the coastal regions, providing a glimpse of older, more traditional ways of life, away from the bustle of the resorts and tourist sites. Unfortunately, mapping is poor, so navigation can be difficult. Be wary of the heat and the sun, especially during the middle of the day. Wear a hat and take plenty of water.

Saklıkent

This 18-km (11-mile) long gorge, so narrow in places that the sun doesn't reach it, makes an appealing day out for more experienced walkers. A wooden boardwalk takes you some of the way, but the walk also involves a little wading and scrambling. Bring a picnic, although there are places to eat should you want them.

✉ Saklıkent, 46km southeast of Fethiye ⌚ 8am–5pm 🚌 *Dolmuş*/minibus to Fethiye

Long-distance trail

The Lycian Way is a 509-km (316-mile) walking trail from Fethiye through the mountains to Antalya. It is clearly marked and there is an accompanying guidebook and excellent website that offer suggestions of where to stay and eat. It is possible to do a small section; the end near Fethiye is easiest; www.lycianway.com.

Watersports and Adventure Tours

Windsurfing, parasailing, jet-skiing and canoeing (➤ 114) are the most popular activities, and snorkelling, under supervision, is enthralling for children. It's wise to check what your travel insurance says about accidents involving watersports.

In the bigger resorts it is worth asking whether the agencies that handle boat trips can also arrange activities such as trekking, canoeing, or rafting. Older children are usually accepted, provided they have an adult with them. Try Borda, Neyzen Tevfir Caddesi 48, Bodrum ☎ 0252 313 7767; www.adventure-yachting.com.

Films

Films originally in English are not usually dubbed, only subtitled in Turkish, and most of the big releases find their way into Turkish cinemas.

Pubs, Clubs, Discos & Bars

The Kuşadası Scene
Barlar Sokaği (Beer St/Pub Lane) has the greatest concentration of pubs and clubs, and appeals especially to young British people. The beer flows and the decibel count remains high until well into the morning. The pubs and clubs in the Kale district, the old part of town, are more interesting in appearance at least, with small courtyards converted into bars and dancing floors. She, Ecstasy, Green Bar and Another Bar are some of the more popular joints.

Pubs & Bars

Northern Aegean

Çanakkale

Akol Roof Bar
The Roof Bar on the top floor of the Akol Hotel (► 100) is the best place to enjoy a cocktail while watching the sun set over the Dardanelles. Depending on your taste, the live popular music will either add to or detract from the overall experience.
Akol Hotel, Kordonboyu
0286 217 9456
7am–midnight

Alesta Bar
There is not really a great deal to do in Çanakkale at night and this cosy little bar offers some diversion. It opens early in the evening but only around midnight does the place tend to liven up with music and chat. It's certainly worth a visit and centrally located in town.
Yalı Caddesi
0286 217 0839
6pm–early morning

İzmir

Windows on the Bay
The 31st floor of the Hilton Hotel provides panoramic views of the largest city on the Aegean coast and its splendid bay. From 6 to 9pm business people unwind here with drinks after work, while from 11pm to closing time the atmosphere is much more fun, with middle-of-the-road pop music played by international bands. There is no cover charge, but they do charge an affordable minimum fee at night.
Gazi Osman Paça Bulvarı
0232 441 6060 **11am–2.30am** **61–63, 116, 110, 112, 150**

Kuşadası

Captain's House Café
A pub and restaurant with a sociable buzz every night, and live music. It's a popular choice with holidaymakers who appreciate the understated Turkish ambience.
Attaturk Caddesi 66
0256 612 1200
9.30am–late

Portobello
At the marina side of town, on the road to the Korumar Hotel, there are outdoor tables and lively disco music inside at the Portobello. Foreign and local beers, including Efes, are drawn from a saxophone at the bar!
Ege Vista Is Merkezi 14
0256 618 1708
2pm–2am

Pub Lane
Paddy's (www.paddysbar.com), Sweet Irish Dream, O'Neill's, Molly Malone's and Kitty O'Shea—no prizes for guessing the country of influence of the drinking dens in this alley that is jam-packed with revellers throughout the summer.
Barlar Sokaşi
Afternoon–late

Selçuk

Don Kişot
There are basically only two bars in Selçuk with a bit of life and atmosphere. Don Kişot is small, with a misguided colour scheme, but lively enough. The other

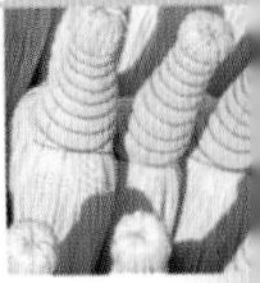

is the Pink Bar, larger and a little more sophisticated, just around the corner.

Sokak 1005 6/A mid-morning–late

Southern Aegean

Bodrum

Second only to Istanbul, Bodrum is heaving with bars and clubs. Dr. Alin Bey Kok and Cumhuriyet Meydanı together make up the local 'bar street'. Start hopping.

Ora

A cavernous, ancient-looking building that usually manages to fill every inch of its floor space with revellers, this is one of the most popular bars in Bodrum. While the slogan of 'the bar where you can dance on the tables' is not always taken literally, it gives a good idea of the atmosphere.

Dr. Alim Bey Caddesi 19/21 0252 614 63903 Mid-morning–late

'Quick Drink Street'

This is the literal translation of Tektekçiler Sokak, a narrow street filled with small wooden chairs and the sound of Turkish music played on traditional instruments. The idea is that one passes through this street, stopping for ten minutes or so to enjoy a drink and take in the music and singing, then moving on to somewhere else.The street is first right after passing the Ora pub.

Tektekçiler Sokak
Early to late evening

Fethiye and Hisarönü

Boozey Bar

This is a no-frills bar with taped music and a snooker table that is popular with English visitors. The place never really goes over the top, but can be relied on to remain convivial and...well, boozy.

Hisarönü 0252 616 6726
11am–late
***Dolmuş*/minibus to Fethiye**

Ottoman Café

It is a little surprising there aren't more pubs like this one along the coast. The interior re-creates, with some imagination, an Ottoman-style atmosphere with the help of antique copper pots adorning the walls and Turkish folk music. The place is sometimes taken over by package groups brought here by tour operators, but it can make a relaxing venue during the afternoon.

Karagözler Caddesi 3/B Fethiye 0252 612 1148
10am–4pm

Clubs & Discos

Northern Aegean

Kuşadası

Emperor

Noisy, popular disco surrounded by bars.

Barlar Sokaği
0256 612 2575
Until late

Southern Aegean

Bodrum

Bodrum Night Club

This very large indoor disco is one of Bodrum's top night spots. The light shows are worth catching. The DJs keep the rock

The Marmaris Scene

Marmaris also has its Beer Street/Pub Lane quarter where pubs and clubs rub shoulders with one another. Predominantly British in character, the area is very noisy, but friendly, with Turkish bands playing Western pop music. Check out, for starters, The Green House, Horizon, Casablanca and the Blue Moon.

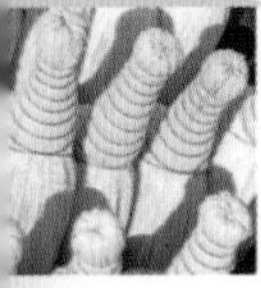

Diving
The British-managed European Diving Centre in Içmler 0252 455 4733 is one of the most professional companies offering certificated diving courses.

music going and maintain a very upbeat atmosphere. Occasional theme nights.
Dr. Alim Bey Caddesi
0252 313 3600; www.clubbodrum.com
7pm–4am

Halikarnas
This legendary outdoor disco is the number one hot-spot in Bodrum. The laser-and-light show, usually around midnight, is spectacular and other diversions come in the form of exotic-looking belly dancers and leather-clad professional dancing groups. The DJs are very good and usually include a well-known personality from Britain.
Cumhuriyet Caddesi
0252 316 8000
8pm– early morning

Jazz Café
This place gets off to a slow start with jazz music early in the evening, but as midnight approaches the music changes and the dancing gets going. Very popular and very lively, even at 4AM.
Paşatarlası Caddesi 9
0252 614 66341
7pm–5am

Fethiye

Car Cemetery Pub
This well-known establishment has a pool table upstairs, cappuccinos and toasted marshmallows early in the evening and cocktails and iced chocolate later. There are more pubs in the immediate vicinity, but the Car Cemetery is always worth a visit.
Karagözler Caddesi
0252 614 2521
4pm–late

Yes!
Run by a Turkish-English couple and attracting a mixture of Turkish and European visitors. Entry is free, happy hour is from 9pm to midnight. The music livens up after 11pm with oldies as well as current favourites. They also host occasional theme nights and dancing shows, include belly dancing.
Cumhuriyet Caddesi 9
0252 614 9289 **8pm–4am**

Music Factory
This is currently the most popular disco for the younger people in Fethiye. The dancing starts around 11pm. There are occasional shows, and professional dancers make effective use of the balcony that surrounds the dance floor.
Hamam Sokak 29 **0252 612 3778** **7.30pm–4am**

Marmaris and Içmeler

Back Street
A long-standing local favourite, this noisy club manages to maintain its popularity through a mix of brash sound and light, great food, a large dance floor, open-air terrace and cocktails.
Bar Street **0252 412 5071** **Until late** ***Dolmuş*/ minibus to Marmaris**

Joy
This is a well-established disco in İçmeler and its circular shape makes it easy to identify. It's on the right side of the main road as you come into İçmeler from Marmaris.
İçmeler **0252 455 3302** **11pm–3am** ***Dolmuş*/ minibus to Marmaris**

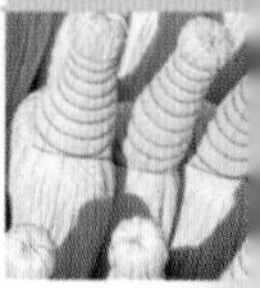

Turkish Baths & Massage

Turkish Bath & Massage

Turkey's fine tradition of a cleansing and sociable bathtime goes back to the influence of the Romans, and a visit to a traditional bath house (*hamam*) is a memorable part of any visit to Turkey. After depositing clothes in a locker you put on a wrap (*peştamal*) and proceed to the main bath area, where an attendant delivers a refreshing body scrub of varying degrees of intensity. Rinsing and shampooing follows, in preparation for the massage. The massage should be on the great slab of marble that dominates the centre of any *hamam*. In a very touristy *hamam* the experience may be disappointingly mild, perhaps because the masseur thinks you might not recover from the full, highly invigorating treatment. If the masseur uses only soap, rather than oil, then it is not the real thing.

The traditional *hamam* has separate days of the week for male and female customers and will use male and female masseurs respectively.

Northern Aegean

Kuşadası

Belediye
Situated across from the old mosque and featuring traditional mixed bathing.
✉ Yildirmit Caddesi ☎ 0256 614 1219 🕐 9am–9pm

Kaleiçi Hamanı
If you fail to make a visit, warns the cute advertisement, 'we will think that you don't like your body'. Located behind the post office.
✉ Camikebir Mah Eyul Sokak 17 ☎ 0256 614 1292 🕐 9am–9pm

Selçuk

Hamam
The *hamam* is in the centre of town, next door to the police station. Mixed bathing and a soft massage.
✉ Sokak 2002 ☎ 0232 892 6198 🕐 Mid-morning–10pm

Southern Aegean

Bodrum

Hamam
This is a more traditional *hamam* than you might expect for Bodrum. Wednesday and Saturday afternoons are women only.
✉ Dere Umucra Sokak 🕐 8am–5pm

Fethiye

Hamam
Although the *hamam* itself dates back to the 16th century, this is a touristy establishment and one that most Turkish people would turn up their noses at.
✉ Hamam Sokak 20 ☎ 0252 614 9318; www.oldturkishbath.com 🕐 7am–midnight

Marmaris

Sultan
Aimed at the tourist market, with women-only and men-only baths as well as a mixed one and a choice of massages.
✉ Taşlik Centre ☎ 0252 413 6850 🕐 8am–midnight

Wrestling
In early summer there are slippery wrestling contests in which oil-covered opponents attempt to keep each other pinned down on their backs for a set time. In winter months, especially in the area around İzmir and Ephesus, there are camel-wrestling events that provide popular entertainment for young and old alike.

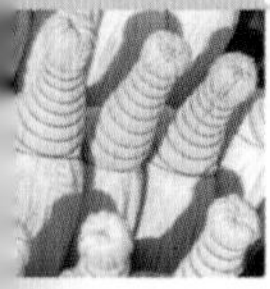

What's On When

Religious Holidays & Festivals

Only a few special days occur at the same time every year in Turkey because they are calculated according to the Muslim lunar calendar. *Kurban Bayramı* is a festival of sacrifice commemorating Abraham's willingness to sacrifice his son Isaac. It is marked by the sacrifice of millions of lambs across the country and the distribution of the meat to those in need. During the month of Ramadan (starting 25 October in 2003), Muslims do not eat, drink or smoke between sunrise and sunset, but this should not cause a problem for anyone travelling along the Aegean coast. The end of Ramadan is celebrated by a festival (*İeker Bayramı*), marked by family get-togethers and the exchanging of sweets.

Local Events

Mid-January to **late February** is the time to watch for camel-wrestling in the Selçuk and Denizli areas.
15 March in Çanakkale is usually marked by special events, commemorating the 1915 victory at sea.
Mid-April sees the İzmir Film Festival, an international festival featuring foreign releases in their own languages.
Late April to **mid-May** sees the Ephesus Festival in and around Selçuk. Music and dancing events take place, although the staging of events in the ancient theatre is currently being affected by the restoration programme.
Mid-May is International Yacht Week in Marmaris when regatta and arts events take place. There is also a yacht race during the first week of November.
The second half of May brings a Jazz Festival to Bodrum (☎ 0252 316 7718).
Mid-June–early July is the time of the International İzmir Festival, with events also taking place at Selçuk and Ephesus.
July and August see Çeşme host a Song and Music competition.
In **August/September**, İzmir hosting its annual International Trade Fair. The practical result of this for non-commercial visitors is that the better hotels, and even restaurants, will be heavily booked.
Early September is the Selçuk Festival, featuring Turkish folk dances and musical events.
November is the second of the two Marmaris International Yacht Race weeks.

Market Days

It is always worth asking at the local tourist office about where and when the weekly market is held. Such market days are important to Turkish people living in the countryside, and the local town will be visibly busier with the influx. Usually there will be an area in town set apart for stalls and, although the merchandise is not targeted at tourists, the scene is still a lively one and worth a visit. Kuşadası is an exception in that the two weekly markets (Tuesday and Friday) are also aimed at tourists. You can get more information at local tourist offices.

Practical Matters

Above: *A proud taxi-driver in Çanakkale; not all taxis are looked after so well*
Right: *In other places the pace of travel is slower*

TIME DIFFERENCES

GMT	Turkey West Coast	Germany	USA (NY)	Netherlands	Spain
12 noon	2pm	1pm	7am	1pm	1pm

BEFORE YOU GO

WHAT YOU NEED

● Required
○ Suggested
▲ Not required

All visitors required a passport with at least six months beyond the date of entry. If you have Turkish nationality, a Turkish ID card will surfice.

	UK	Germany	USA	Netherlands	Spain
Passport or National Identity Card where applicable	●	●	●	●	●
Visa (obtainable on arrival—check regulations before your journey))	●	▲	●	●	●
Onward or Return Ticket	○	○	○	○	○
Health Inoculations	▲	▲	▲	▲	▲
Health Documentation (Health, ➤ 123)	▲	▲	▲	▲	▲
Travel Insurance	○	○	○	○	○
Driving Licence (EU or International)	●	●	●	●	●
Car Insurance Certificate (if own car)	●	●	●	●	●
Car registration document (if own car)	●	●	●	●	●

WHEN TO GO

Turkey's West Coast

High season
Low season

JAN	FEB	MAR	APR	MAY	JUN	JUL	AUG	SEP	OCT	NOV	DEC
Low season	Low season	Low season	High season	High season	High season	High season	High season	High season	High season	Low season	Low season
13°C	14°C	17°C	21°C	25°C	30°C	34°C	34°C	31°C	26°C	19°C	14°C
Sunshine & showers	Sunshine & showers	Sunshine & showers	Sun	Sun	Sun	Sun	Sun	Sun	Sun	Sunshine & showers	Sunshine & showers

Sun
Sunshine & showers

TOURIST OFFICES

In the UK
Turkish Information Office
First Floor, Egyptian House
170–3 Piccadilly
London WIV 9DD
☎ 020 7629 7771
Fax: 020 7491 0773
www.gototurkey.co.uk

In the USA
Turkish Information Office
821 United Nations Plaza
New York
NY 10017
☎ 212/687 2194
Fax: 212/599 7568
www.tourismturkey.com

2525 Massachusetts Ave
NW
Washington DC
20036
☎ 202/612 6800
Fax: 202/319 7446

POLICE 155

JANDARMA (IN COUNTRY AREAS) 156

FIRE 110

AMBULANCE 112

WHEN YOU ARE THERE

ARRIVING

Turkish Airlines has scheduled flights to İzmir via Istanbul from major European cities, and onwards to all domestic airports in Turkey including İzmir, Dalaman and Bodrum. During the tourist season direct charter flights fly to resort areas. Ferry services operate from Italy, and from many Greek islands..

Adnan Menderes Airport
Kilometres to İzmir

25km (16 miles)

Journey times

Train	N/A
Bus	30 minutes
Car	20 minutes

Bodrum Airport
Kilometres to Bodrum

50km (31 miles)

Journey times

Train	N/A
Bus	40 minutes
Car	50 minutes

MONEY

Turkey changed its currency in 2004, knocking off many noughts. The currency is the Yeni Turk Lira (YTL; new Turkish Lira) which was, at the time of writing, roughly equivalent in value to the euro. Coins (kuruş) are in 1, 5, 10, 20, and 1 YTL denominations. Notes are in 1, 5, 10, 20, 50 and 100YTL units. ATMs are everywhere and credit cards widely accepted. Travellers' cheques attrac t a discretionary commission if cashed at banks. Nobody refuses cash and most tourist shops will quote in lira, euros, US dollars or pounds.

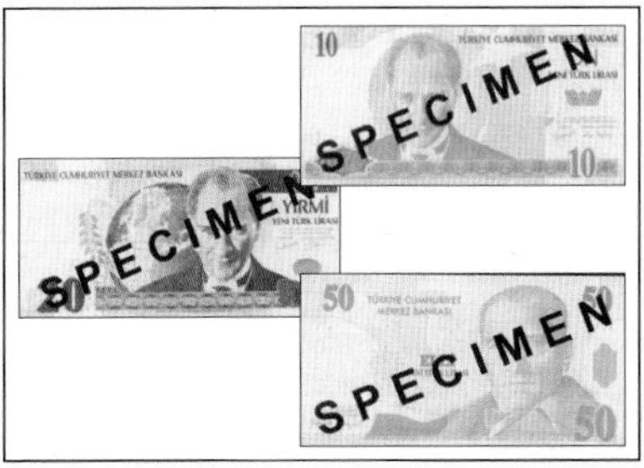

TIME

Local time is 2 hours ahead of Greenwich Mean Time (GMT+2) but daylight saving (GMT+3) operates between late March and late September.

CUSTOMS

YES

Limited amounts of alcohol, cigarettes and coffee may be brought into the country.

Liquor (wine or spirits): 5 litres
Cigarettes: 200
Cigars: 50
Tobacco: 200g
Coffee: 1.5kg
Tea: 500gm
Chocolate: 1kg; sweets: 1kg
Perfume: 5 bottles (each 120ml max)
Toilet water: no limit

Airports have duty free facilities at entry points; some are open 24 hours.

No more than US$5,000-worth of Turkish lira may be exported. Personal electronic goods, laptops and mobile phones can be brought with you.

NO

Drugs, firearms, ammunition, offensive weapons, obscene material and unlicensed animals. Smuggling of drugs carries extreme penalities.

EMBASSIES AND CONSULATES

UK	Germany	USA	Netherlands	Spain
(0232) 463 5151	(0232) 421 6995	(0232) 421 3643	(0232) 463 4960	(0232) 489 7936

WHEN YOU ARE THERE

TOURIST OFFICES

- Bodrum
  Bariş Meydanı 48
  ☎ 0252 316 1091
- Çanakkale
  Next to main dock
  ☎ 0217 0286 1187
- Fethiye
  İskele Karşısı 1
  ☎ 0252 614 1527
- İzmir
  Akdeniz Mah, 1344 Sok
  No.2, Pasaport
  ☎ 0232 483 6216/483 5117;
  www.izmir.turizm.gov.tr
- Kuşadası
  Liman Caddesi
  ☎ 0256 614 1103
- Marmaris
  İskele Meydanı 2
  ☎ 0252 313 0722
- Selçuk
  Atatürk Mah,
  EfesMüzesi Karşısı 23
  ☎ 0232 892 1328;
  www.selcuk.gov.tr

There are also tourist offices in most towns of interest: see individual entries for addresses and telephone numbers.

NATIONAL HOLIDAYS

J	F	M	A	M	J	J	A	S	O	N	D
1			1	1			1		1		

1 Jan	New Year's Day
23 Apr	Independence Day
19 May	Atatürk Commemoration Youth and Sports Day
30 Aug	Commemoration of the Turkish victory over the Greeks in 1922
29 Oct	Commemoration of the Proclamation of the Republic in 1923

Moveable Holidays
Islamic holidays, the dates of which change from year to year, are also recognised in most of Turkey (see ➤ 116).

OPENING HOURS

- ○ Shops
- ● Offices
- ● Banks
- ● Archaeological Sites
- ● Museums/Monuments
- ● Pharmacies

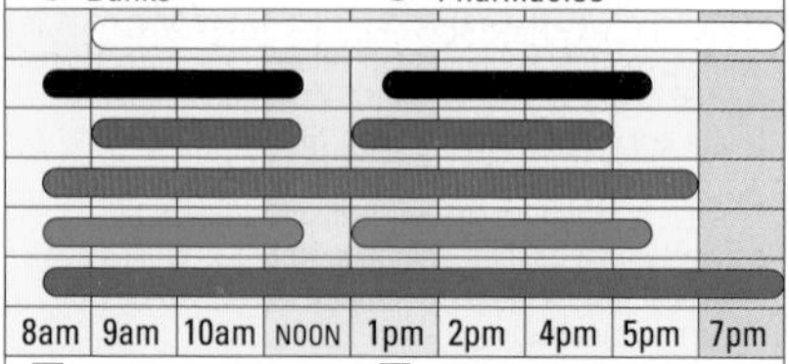

☐ Day ☐ Midday ☐ Evening

In addition to the times shown above, shops in tourist areas may open earlier and stay open for much longer, sometimes until midnight, every day of the week. Banks are closed on Saturdays and Sundays. Most have ATM machines with 24-hour access. Museums are usually closed on Mondays.

Major post offices open Mon–Sat 8am–midnight, Sun 9–7. Minor post offices open Mon–Fri 8.30–12.30, 1.30–3.30. Many fuel stations open 24 hours, seven days a week.

DRIVE ON THE **RIGHT**

TOILETS **CHARGE**

PUBLIC TRANSPORT

Internal Flights Turkish Airlines operate domestic flights connecting Istanbul, Ankara and most of Turkey's major cities with the airports at Dalaman, İzmir and Bodrum. Onur Air, Atlas Air and Fly Air operate low-flights between main Turkish hubs.

Trains There is a very limited, and usually very slow, train service covering a small area of western Turkey, and few visitors use it. From İzmir, trains run to Selçuk, Denizli and Manisa. For reservations ☎ 0232 484 5353; for information 0232 484 8638.

Buses Buses are the most popular and practical means of getting around. The service is usually very reliable and professional. Tickets can be purchased at the bus station (*otogar*), in advance, and usually on the actual bus if you board after the starting point. Smoking is not allowed on buses.

Boat Trips The best way to see the coastline, and to reach otherwise inaccessible coves, is by boat. In all the major resorts, boat operators will be found at the harbour. Longer cruises with a crew, lasting 3–7 days, are especially popular from Bodrum and Marmaris. Ferries to Greek islands are commonplace.

***Dolmuş*/minibus** A *dolmuş* is a shared taxi. You pay according to the distance travelled and can get on or off anywhere along the route. For most travel in the region, the *dolmuş* is a minibus and you pay on board. For local travel between villages or small towns it is the best means of transport.

CAR RENTAL

Leading international car rental companies have offices in İzmir and all of the larger resorts. Many visitors book their car hire in advance from their home country. Drivers must be over 21 and have a valid driving licence.

TAXIS

Taxis are usually yellow, and can be hailed from the pavement or from ranks in the major resorts. Fares may be metered, but agreeing on a price beforehand is common practice. Fares double between midnight and 6AM.

DRIVING

Speed limit on motorways: **120kph/74.4mph**

Speed limit in open areas: **90kph/55.8mph**

Speed limit in towns: **50kph/31mph**

Seat belts must be worn in front seats at all times and in rear seats where fitted.

There is a total ban on alcohol when driving. Random tests are quite common and police will issue on-the-spot fines.

Fuel stations sell super and normal fuel (*benzin*), diesel (*mazot*) and unleaded fuel (*kursunşuz*). The price of fuel is extremely high. Credit cards are accepted. Service stations often have good toilets and are full service.

If you break down driving your own car, call the Turkish Touring and Automobile Club (☎ Istanbul 0212 282 8140; fax 0212 282 8042; www.turing.org.tr). If your car is hired, follow the instructions you were given when hiring the vehicle. All accidents must be reported to the police. Don't move your car.

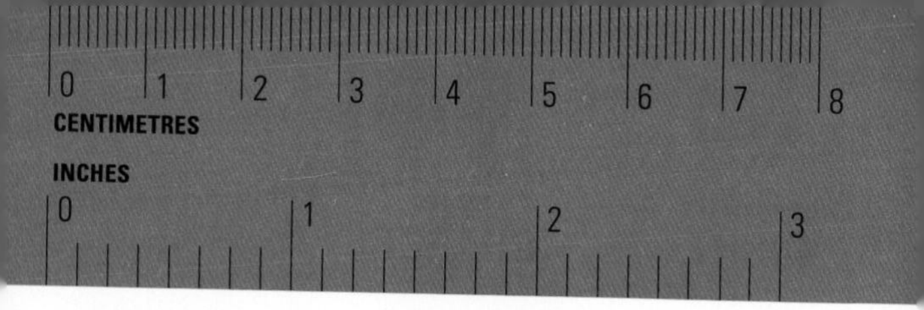

PERSONAL SAFETY

The everyday police force in towns have blue uniforms. There are special tourist police in the major resorts who look the same but who should be able to speak some English and/or German.
To help prevent crime:

- Do not carry more cash than you need
- Do not leave valuables on the beach or at the poolside
- Use safe boxes in your hotel
- Never leave anything of value in your car

Police assistance:
☎ **155**
from any call box

TELEPHONES

There are pay-phones on many streets, and at PTT offices. Phonecards are sold at post offices and newsagents. Most phones also accept credit cards. Main European mobile phones can be used here; North American visitors will need tri-band. Internet cafés are everywhere.

International Dialling Codes	
From Turkey to:	
UK:	**00 44**
Germany:	**00 49**
USA & Canada:	**00 1**
Netherlands:	**00 31**
Spain:	**00 34**

POST

Post offices (PTT) are easily recognisable by a black-on-yellow logo. In major resorts and larger towns the main PTT will stay open for phone calls until midnight. Open: 8am–7/8pm. Closed Sat pm and Sun. Stamps are usually also available where postcards are sold.

ELECTRICITY

The power supply in Turkey is 220 volts.
Sockets take two round pin plugs but there are two sizes in use. Bring your own adaptor. Travellers from the USA will need a transformer. Power cuts are frequent in rural areas but usually short lived.

TIPS/GRATUITIES

Yes ✓ No ✕		
Restaurants (service not inc)	✓	10%
Cafés/bar (if service not inc.)	✓	change
Tour Guides	✓	10–15%
Hairdressers	✓	change
Taxis	✓	round up fare
Chambermaids	✓	1.5–2YTL
Hotel porters	✓	1.5–2YTL
Cloakroom attendants/toilets	✓	50 kuruş
Petrol-pump attendants	✓	Small change

What to photograph: archaeological sites, villages, harbours and sunsets.
What not to photograph: anything to do with the military.
When to photograph: the summer sun can be powerful the height of the day, making photographs sometimes appear too 'flat'; early morning or late evening is a better time.
Where to buy films: film and camera batteries are readily available from tourist shops in the main resorts. Most larger photographic shops will process digital photographs.

HEALTH

Insurance

Arrange travel insurance in your home country before arriving in Turkey. Turkey is not a member of the EU, so EU visitors cannot obtain free medical treatment. Where there are reciprocal agreements you generally need to pay first then get reimbursed.

Dental Services

Dental treatment must be paid for. Check your travel insurance to see whether, and to what extent, dental treatment is covered.

Sun Advice

The sunniest and hottest months are July, August and September, with an average of twelve hours of sunshine and temperatures in the low 30s°C. During these months especially you should avoid the midday sun and use a strong sunblock and always drink plenty of water.

Drugs

Prescription and non-prescription drugs and medicines are available from pharmacies (*eczane*). They are able to dispense many drugs that would normally be available only on prescription in many countries.

Safe Water

Tap water is generally safe to drink, though it can be heavily chlorinated and taste unpleasant. Mineral water is inexpensive and is sold either sparkling (*maden suyu*) or still (*memba suyu*).

CONCESSIONS

Most sights offer discounts for children. Holders of an International Student Identity Card (ISIC) may be able to obtain some concessions on travel and entrance fees and passengers with disabilities get a substantial discount on trains. There is the occasional hostel where an ISIC card is helpful. Inexpensive accommodation is also available in pensions (*pansiyons*).

On the whole, concessions are few and far between and apply only to native Turks.

CLOTHING SIZES

Turkey	UK	Europe	USA	
46	36	46	36	Suits
48	38	48	38	
50	40	50	40	
52	42	52	42	
54	44	54	44	
56	46	56	46	
41	7	41	8	Shoes
42	7.5	42	8.5	
43	8.5	43	9.5	
44	9.5	44	10.5	
45	10.5	45	11.5	
46	11	46	12	
37	14.5	37	14.5	Shirts
38	15	38	15	
39/40	15.5	39/40	15.5	
41	16	41	16	
42	16.5	42	16.5	
43	17	43	17	
36	8	34	6	Dresses
38	10	36	8	
40	12	38	10	
42	14	40	12	
44	16	42	14	
46	18	44	16	
38	4.5	38	6	Shoes
38	5	38	6.5	
39	5.5	39	7	
39	6	39	7.5	
40	6.5	40	8	
41	7	41	8.5	

WHEN DEPARTING

- Confirm your flight departure one or two days before leaving.
- Remaining Turkish currency is of little use and small amounts will not easily be exchanged in your own country.
- Departure tax is usually paid for when you purchase your ticket but check that this is so in your case.

LANGUAGE

Turkish, loosely related to Finnish and Hungarian, is an extremely difficult language that builds sentences by adding suffixes to the basic word, and keeps the verb at the end. This can also alter the structure of the basic word and make it virtually unrecognisable to the untrained eye. Pronunciation *ai/ay* long i, eg side; *c* a hard j, eg jam; *ç* ch, eg chat; *ı* er/uh, eg letter; *ğ* y; *ü* ew, eg few (roughly); *ö* ur (more like the Scandinanvian ø); *j* zh (no English equivalent); *ş* sh, eg shut.sh, eg shut.

hotel	*otel*	bath	*banyo*
pension	*pansiyon*	shower	*duş*
single room	*tek kişilik oda*	toilet	*tuvalet*
double room	*iki kişilik oda*	hot water	*sıcak su*
one night	*bir gecelik*	key	*anahtar*
reservation	*reservasyon*	lift	*asansör*
room service	*oda servisi*	sea view	*deniz manzarası*
towel	*havlu*	reception	*resepsiyon*

bank	*banka*	credit card	*kredi kart*
exchange office	*döriz*	exchange rate	*döviz kuru*
post office	*PTT or postane*	commission charge	*komisyon ücreti*
stamp	*pul*	cashier	*kasiyer*
cheque	*çeki*	change	*bozuk para*
traveller's cheque	*seyahat çeki*	foreign currency	*doviz*

restaurant	*lokanta/restoran*	fruit	*meyva*
bill	*hesap*	bread	*ekmek*
breakfast	*kahvaltı*	beer	*bira*
appetisers/ vegetable in olive oil	*meze/ zeytinyağlılar*	wine	*şarap*
		ice	*buz*
		water	*su*
dessert	*tatlı*	mineral water	*maden suyu*
yoghurt drink	*ayran*	coffee	*kahve*
tea	*çay*	milk	*süt*

aeroplane	*uçak*	return	*gidiş-dönüş*
airport	*havaalanı*	port	*liman*
train station	*istasyon*	car	*araba*
bus	*otobüs*	taxi	*taksi*
bus station	*otogar*	how do I get to...?	*...'a/e nasil giderim?*
boat	*vapur/feribot*		
ferry landing	*iskele*	how far is..?	*...ne kadar uzak?*
a ticket to...	*...'a bir bilet*	where is...?	*...nerede?*

yes	*evet*	goodbye	*güle güle* (said by the one staying)
no	*hayır, yok*		
please	*lütfen*	good morning	*günaydin*
thank you	*teşekkür ederim, mersi, sağol*	good afternoon	*iyi günler*
		goodnight	*iyi geceler*
hello	*merhaba*	sorry	*pardon*
goodbye	*allahaısmarladık* (said by the one leaving)	how much?	*ne kadar/kaça?*
		open/closed	*açık/kapalı*
		excuse me	*özür dilerim*
you're welcome	*bir şey değil*	where?	*nerede?*

INDEX

Acknowledgements

Sean Sheehan would like to thank Hulya Soylu, Hasim Akçura, Arzu Akalay, Leyla Cingöz, Ms Goneng, Nebaha Arabaci and A Soames for their help with his enquiries.

The Automobile Association wishes to thank the following photographers and libraries for their assistance in the preparation of this book.

MARY EVANS PICTURE LIBRARY 14b; MRI BANKERS GUIDE TO FOREIGN CURRENCY 119; ROBERT HARDING PICTURE LIBRARY 68, 77; NATURE PHOTOGRAPHERS LTD 12 (K Carlson), 40 (P Craig-Cooper), 49 (P R Sterry); PICTURES COLOUR LIBRARY 62b; SPECTRUM COLOUR LIBRARY 10/1, 26b, 89b

The remaining photographs are held in the Association's own photo library (AA PHOTO LIBRARY) and were taken by Jean-François Pin with the exception of the following: F/cover (b) boy, (f) carpet seller, (h) fresh fish salad, 90b taken by Pete Bennett; 82b taken by Steve Day; B/cover Medusa carving, 5b, 6b, 6c, 8c, 9c, 11, 13, 15a, 16a, 17a, 18a, 19a, 20a, 20b, 21a, 22a, 22b, 23a, 22/3, 24a, 25a, 26a, 31c, 32b, 36b, 39b, 41b, 44, 45, 46, 47b, 48, 50, 51a, 52b, 55b, 60b, 64/5, 65, 69b, 71a, 74, 75, 76, 80a, 81b, 83, 86b, 86c, 88, 91a, 92, 93, 94, 95, 96, 97, 98, 99, 100, 101, 102, 103, 104, 105, 106, 107, 108, 109, 110, 111, 112, 113, 114, 115, 116, 117b, 122c taken by Paul Kenward; 15b, 16b, 24b taken by Dario Mitideri and F/cover (a) tea, 70b, 87b which were taken by Tony Souter.

Revision management: Apostrophe S Limited

Page layout: Barfoot Design

Dear Essential Traveller

Your comments, opinions and recommendations are very important to us. So please help us to improve our travel guides by taking a few minutes to complete this simple questionnaire.

You do not need a stamp (unless posted outside the UK). If you do not want to cut this page from your guide, then photocopy it or write your answers on a plain sheet of paper.

Send to: **The Editor, AA World Travel Guides, FREEPOST SCE 4598, Basingstoke RG21 4GY.**

Your recommendations...

We always encourage readers' recommendations for restaurants, nightlife or shopping – if your recommendation is used in the next edition of the guide, we will send you a ***FREE* AA *Essential* Guide** of your choice. Please state below the establishment name, location and your reasons for recommending it.

____

____

____

____

Please send me **AA *Essential*** __________________________

About this guide...

Which title did you buy?
AA *Essential* ________________________________
Where did you buy it? ______________________________
When? m m / y y

Why did you choose an AA *Essential* Guide? ____________________

____

____

____

____

Did this guide meet your expectations?
Exceeded ☐ Met all ☐ Met most ☐ Fell below ☐
Please give your reasons ____________________________

____

____

____

continued on next page...

Were there any aspects of this guide that you particularly liked? ___________

____

____

Is there anything we could have done better? ___________________

____

____

About you...

Name (*Mr/Mrs/Ms*) ______________________________

Address ______________________________

____

______________________ Postcode ______________

Daytime tel nos ______________________________

Please only give us your mobile phone number if you wish to hear from us about other products and services from the AA and partners by text or mms.

Which age group are you in?

Under 25 ☐ 25–34 ☐ 35–44 ☐ 45–54 ☐ 55–64 ☐ 65+ ☐

How many trips do you make a year?

Less than one ☐ One ☐ Two ☐ Three or more ☐

Are you an AA member? Yes ☐ No ☐

About your trip...

When did you book? m m / y y When did you travel? m m / y y

How long did you stay? ______________________________

Was it for business or leisure? ______________________________

Did you buy any other travel guides for your trip?

If yes, which ones? ______________________________

Thank you for taking the time to complete this questionnaire. Please send it to us as soon as possible, and remember, you do not need a stamp (*unless posted outside the UK*).

Happy Holidays!

The information we hold about you will be used to provide the products and services requested and for identification, account administration, analysis, and fraud/loss prevention purposes. More details about how that information is used is in our privacy statement, which you'll find under the heading "Personal Information" in our terms and conditions and on our website: www.theAA.com. Copies are also available from us by post, by contacting the Data Protection Manager at AA, Southwood East, Apollo Rise, Farnborough, Hampshire GU14 OJW.

We may want to contact you about other products and services provided by us, or our partners (by mail, telephone) but please tick the box if you DO NOT wish to hear about such products and services from us by mail or telephone. ☐